Call Center Succes

Essential Skills for CSRs

Lloyd C. Finch

A Fifty-Minute™ Series Book

Call Center Success

Essential Skills for CSRs

Lloyd C. Finch

Credits:
Senior Editor: **Debbie Woodbury**
Editor: **Hanna Hurley**
Copy Editor: **Charlotte Bosarge**
Production Manager: **Judy Petry**
Design: **Amy Shayne**
Production Artist: **Carol Lindahl**
Cartoonist: **Ralph Mapson**

Printed in the United States of America by Von Hoffmann Graphics, Inc.

CrispLearning.com

01 02 03 10 9 8 7 6 5 4 3 2

Library of Congress Catalog Card Number 00-105371
Finch, Lloyd C.
Call Center Success
ISBN 1-56052-578-9

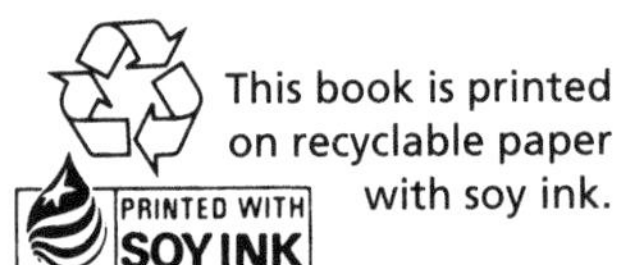

This book is printed on recyclable paper with soy ink.

Learning Objectives For:

CALL CENTER SUCCESS

The objectives for *Call Center Success: Essential Skills for CSRs* are listed below. They have been developed to guide you, the reader, to the core issues covered in this book.

THE OBJECTIVES OF THIS BOOK ARE:

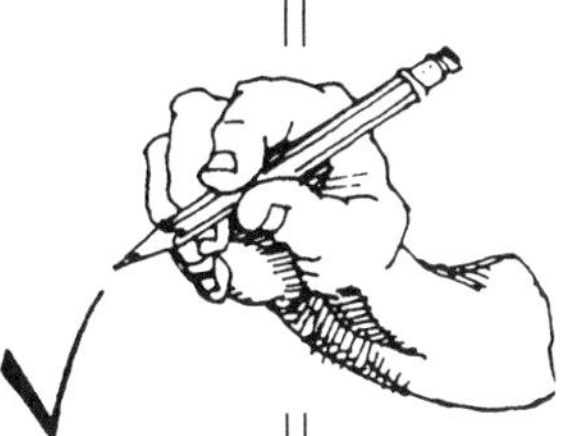

- ❑ 1) To explain the basics of providing high quality customer service
- ❑ 2) To describe the six elements of professionalism
- ❑ 3) To explore how to understand and respond to customer needs
- ❑ 4) To provide techniques for building effective communication skills
- ❑ 5) To discuss the importance of a positive attitude
- ❑ 6) To describe how to create and use a self-improvement plan

ASSESSING YOUR PROGRESS

In addition to the learning objectives, Crisp Learning has developed an **assessment** that covers the fundamental information presented in this book. A twenty-five item, multiple choice/true-false questionnaire allows the reader to evaluate his or her comprehension of the subject matter. An answer sheet with a chart matching the questions to the listed objectives is also available. To learn how to obtain a copy of this assessment please call **1-800-442-7477** and ask to speak with a Customer Service Representative.

Assessments should not be used in any selection process.

Preface

Welcome to *Call Center Success: Essential Skills for CSRs*. This book includes important customer service skills a Customer Service Representative (CSR) needs to satisfy customers. When you apply the skills, ideas, and suggestions included in this book, two important changes will occur. First, your job will become easier, and second, you will become a skilled CSR professional.

Call Center Success will increase your understanding of the challenges, skills, and competencies needed to succeed in a call center. Working in a call center is a fast-paced, demanding job. With the growth of e-commerce, tech support, and other customer service opportunities, the future for Customer Service Reps is bright. Reps who can provide outstanding service will be highly sought, valuable employees.

Lloyd C. Finch

About the Author

Lloyd Finch is President of Alpha Consulting Group, a company devoted to customer service improvement training and the development of customer service training products. Lloyd is an experienced speaker on customer service issues. Prior to forming Alpha consulting he had extensive sales, customer service, and sales management experience in an 18-year career with Pacific Bell and AT&T. Lloyd may be reached at 831-624-5288. His email is ALPHACONSULTING@prodigy.net

Other books by the author are *Telephone Courtesy & Customer Service*, *Twenty Ways to Improve Customer Service*, and *Success as a CSR*, by Crisp Publications, Inc.

Contents

Part 4: Building Your Communication Skills

Part 5: Attitude–Your Most Important Asset

Part 6: A Plan for Self Improvement

P A R T 1

The CSR—A Powerful Voice

The CSR's Valuable Role

The Customer Service Representative (CSR) is the voice of the organization. As the customer's primary contact, the CSR projects the company's image and plays a critical role in building customer relationships. To carry out this demanding assignment, a CSR has multiple responsibilities. A successful rep must handle a high volume of calls, respond quickly and accurately to customers' needs, and present a high level of professionalism at all times.

A CSR must possess numerous skills and attributes to be successful in this demanding profession. Some of the skills and attributes include:

- ➤ The ability to provide quality service on every call
- ➤ The expertise to accurately assess the type of customer on a call
- ➤ The talent to communicate effectively with customers
- ➤ A positive attitude that transmits to customers, co-workers, and managers

These skills, as well as others, make the CSR's job manageable. With some practice and training, reps can quickly add these skills to their collection of useful effective customer service tools. Learning these skills will:

- ➤ Make an extremely demanding job less difficult
- ➤ Reduce on-the-job stress
- ➤ Increase customer satisfaction
- ➤ Project a positive company image

First Impressions Count

In the typical call center, a CSR gets only one chance to satisfy the customer. When the customer makes a specific request, the CSR must satisfy it or arrange a follow-up call. This same customer may call several times with other inquiries, but it's rare that the same rep will talk to that customer again.

In other customer service situations, a CSR may have frequent contact with the same customer. These ongoing exchanges allow a relationship to build. At times, this relationship is even strong enough for errors. For example, suppose during the customer's first contact, the rep makes a mistake. In the next exchange the rep apologizes and corrects the earlier error. But in a call center environment, the rep usually doesn't get this second chance.

Many call centers document each customer call. This practice allows the next CSR who talks with the customer to know what transpired on previous calls. When documenting this type of information, brevity and accuracy are key. If the details of a customer problem aren't entered accurately the next CSR who speaks with that customer may be caught short of important background information. Incomplete or inaccurate information diminishes the customer satisfaction and undermines the company's credibility.

When customers encounter knowledgeable, professional, customer-focused reps, their perception of your organization becomes a positive one. If the customer's experience is less than satisfactory, the perception is negative. It's that simple.

The Call Center Challenge

The call center is a demanding place to work. Within the confines of a short customer telephone conversation, a rep must manage the customer conversation, satisfy the needs of the customer, control the length of the call, and upon completion be prepared to immediately take the next call and repeat the process. Additionally, each call is a "blind" call, meaning the rep doesn't know who is calling or what the need is until the customer begins the conversation.

Mix together the management of a high volume of customer calls and the need to be current on new product, service, and policy information and you have the recipe for a very taxing job.

The CSR's success is partially dependent on how well he or she copes with this pressure and stress. Some CSRs seem to roll with the strain, but most are affected to some extent. Managing stress is an essential skill for CSRs. We will explore this further in Part 5: Attitude–Your Most Important Asset, where you will find valuable tips and techniques for maintaining a positive attitude and managing stress.

The Quality Call

Customer Service Reps may take hundreds of calls each day. On each of these calls, the CSR must make sure that the call is of high quality.

A quality call includes:

- ➤ Satisfying customer needs
- ➤ Professionally managing the call
- ➤ Extending courteous service
- ➤ Providing accurate information
- ➤ Controlling the length of the call
- ➤ Demonstrating excellent product and service knowledge

These and other essential skills for professional CSRs are explored in the next section.

P A R T **2**

Gaining the Professional Edge

Six Elements of Professionalism

CSRs are responsible for managing a high volume of calls and providing quality service on each call. Sounds like a balancing act doesn't it? It is! To become a professional CSR, reps must master these six elements.

1. **Manage the customer call**
2. **Know your products and services**
3. **Be a team player**
4. **Remain customer focused**
5. **Take responsibility**
6. **Make a commitment**

ELEMENT 1: Manage the Customer Call

Every customer call is an opportunity to manage the conversation successfully and satisfy the customer.

To manage the customer call, the CSR needs

- ➤ To be prepared
- ➤ To have excellent product and service knowledge
- ➤ A generous amount of common courtesy
- ➤ To be a good listener
- ➤ To have a good attitude
- ➤ To manage the length of the customer call
- ➤ To balance the customer's interest with that of your organization

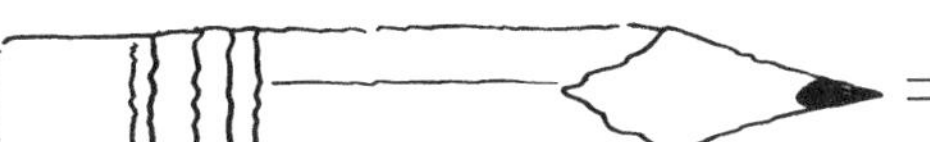

IDENTIFYING CUSTOMER NEEDS QUICKLY

This exercise helps you manage the length of the customer call. By focusing on the customer's need quickly, you can decrease the call duration.

Customer 1: "This is the third time I've called in the last few weeks. Last time I talked to Jorge. He said he would get my bill straightened out. Now, I noticed in your catalog there's a sale that started on the first. If it's still going on I would like to buy a few things. Most of them are on pages 37 and 38. Do you need the item numbers or can I just describe them to you? That's something you guys should fix...these item numbers are almost too small for me to read. They need to be made bigger."

How well did you listen to the customer? The customer's needs are: (circle all that apply)

A. Wants to discuss the billing.

B. Wants to talk to Jorge.

C. Wants to buy a few items from pages 37 and 38.

D. Wants to know if the sale is still on.

E. Wants to discuss the item numbers.

Customer 2: "I hope you can help me. I paid my credit card balance on the 3rd even though it wasn't due until the 10th, but that payment doesn't show on my most recent bill. I may have paid my wife's bill by mistake, but I can't be sure. I thought our account with you was a joint thing...you know, the same credit card number. By the way, I got that insertion in the last bill, about the unicycle. I can't believe you guys are offering a unicycle."

This customer is a little confused, but if you listened closely his immediate need is clear. Circle the best answer.

A. The customer wants to know if his wife is on his account.

B. Wants to know if his check was received and credited.

C. Customer 2 needs a bill explanation.

D. Wants to know if he paid his wife's bill.

E. All of above

Answer Key: Identifying Customer Needs Quickly

Customer 1:
If you listened closely, the customer's need is clear and can be addressed immediately. The customer wants to know if the sale is still on (D) and, if it is, he has an order to place for items on pages 37 and 38 (C).

Customer 2:
"All of the above" is the appropriate answer for this customer. Resolving all the billing issues will probably take some time. But, it is still important to focus on the immediate need of explaining the bill. Getting sidetracked into a discussion about unicycles would only increase the call length.

ELEMENT 2: Know Your Products and Services

To be prepared to manage any customer call, you must have excellent product and service knowledge. The more you know about your products and services the easier it will be to help customers and the less time it will take. When you don't have to do research or ask co-workers or supervisors for input, calls progress more quickly and customer satisfaction increases.

For most reps, developing and maintaining excellent product and service knowledge takes time. Although co-workers and supervisors are available to help you, it is important that you become self-sufficient. Here is an example of what happens when a rep doesn't spend time learning about the products and services offered.

ITC Tech Center relies on strong teamwork. When a CSR can't answer a customer's question or needs assistance, he puts his hand up and a supervisor or co-worker will come over to help. Harry, a CSR, acquired the nickname "Harry the Hand" because his hand was always in the air. Harry is rarely prepared and when he needs the latest information—usually in the middle of call—he puts his hand up. Harry thinks he's a funny, likable guy, but the other CSRs are tired of spending their valuable time assisting him. Harry's average call length is nearly twice as long as everyone else's. This contributes to a long hold time for many customers. To make the problem worse, some of Harry's customers have complained about his lack of knowledge. "Harry the Hand" needs to spend time learning about his products and services. Don't you agree?

How Well Do You Know Your Products and Services?

Rate yourself on the following items on a 1 to 5. Be honest with yourself–this exercise is intended to help you focus on areas for self-improvement.

1 = Poor 2 = Fair 3 = Average 4 = Good 5 = Excellent

__________ **My ability to stay current on product and service offerings.**

__________ **My understanding of our product and service policies.**

__________ **How well I keep up with the latest updates and promotions.**

__________ **My overall product/service knowledge.**

__________ **My ability to easily explain products and services to customers.**

__________ **My ability to handle the commonly asked customer questions.**

__________ **My ability to resolve the most common problems of my customers.**

If you want to be a successful call center rep, you *must* have excellent product and service knowledge. With a high level of knowledge your customers will be more satisfied, call length becomes more manageable, your job becomes easier, and you will experience less stress. Your should aim to have only ratings of 4 and above. Can you do it? Sure you can!

ELEMENT 3: Be a Team Player

In successful call centers a strong sense of teamwork can be seen and felt. The sharing of information is an unspoken rule, accepted by all. New hires need help so everyone helps them. When new information arrives, it's shared with everyone. When a rep is struggling with a response, someone intervenes.

The Non-Team Player

Susan had been working in the call center for three years. An opening for a unit supervisor became available and Susan interviewed for the position. During the interview, the call center manager told Susan that he had noticed she did not share information readily or help other CSRs. Susan didn't have an answer. The manager asked Susan whether she had helped the new hires in her work unit. Susan couldn't answer yes. The manager then asked if she felt she was supportive of the other reps. Susan explained that her job had little to do with teamwork. She said; "It's really me and our customers." Susan was asked about the leadership example she set by not sharing information or helping other CSRs. Susan said she didn't see that as her responsibility.

Teamwork is essential for call center success. Team-oriented reps:

- ➤ Collaborate to solve problems
- ➤ Share information
- ➤ Support co-workers
- ➤ Help new hires

ELEMENT 4: Remain Customer Focused

A rep's foremost responsibility is staying customer focused. During changes and busy times, it's easy to neglect the call center's primary purpose: *satisfy the customer.*

Every change in your customer service structure, policies, products, or services impacts the customer. Successful reps consider how the customer will be affected.

Karen and Mike took on the responsibility of explaining to their work unit the new pricing. Although most items increased in price, a few decreased. At the conclusion of their presentation Zach, a CSR, had these questions: "How do you suggest I explain these changes to my customers? Are there any benefits I should mention? If a customer is upset over the increases, how do I justify them?"

Zach asked some valid questions. Karen and Mike weren't prepared with answers because they were focused only on the pricing, not on the impact the changes would have upon their customers. Zach was more customer focused.

Being customer focused means acting as the customer's advocate. Within your organization, someone must represent the customer's interests. The person closest to the customer is the rep–not the supervisors or managers. As a CSR, you must keep your organization abreast of what the customers are saying, doing, and feeling.

You must also balance the needs of the customer with the interests of the organization. This can be especially challenging when the two do not seem to be aligned. However, keep in mind that satisfied customers are *always* in a business's best interest. Use good judgment in meeting customer needs while also honoring the policies and procedures that allow your organization to remain successful. Exercising good judgment and making effective decisions are essential skills for CSRs.

Customer Advocate or Judgment Error?

Jenny explained the new pricing to a customer. The customer was upset because of the impact the new costs would have on her small business. Jenny explained that the costs of doing business had increased and her organization had to make changes. The customer told Jenny she had not received any notice of a price increase and she wanted the old prices for her order. Jenny explained that the pricing change was announced 30 days ago. The customer said, "I didn't see it and I want the old prices for this order." Jenny told the customer she would see what she could do. Jenny talked with her supervisor who said no. She talked with the call center manager who also said no. Jenny's supervisor was upset that Jenny discussed the problem with the manager and questioned her judgment. Jenny explained, "I was just trying to be the customer's advocate."

Was Jenny being the customer's advocate? Or did Jenny make a judgment error. Check (✔) all the statements below that you think apply.

1. ❑ Jenny should not have tried to get an exception for her customer.
2. ❑ Jenny wasted some valuable time.
3. ❑ Jenny should have politely told the customer that she couldn't offer the old prices.
4. ❑ Jenny was right in trying to get the old prices for her customer.
5. ❑ Once the supervisor said no, Jenny should have stopped her effort.

Here's one answer: Every situation and organization is different but Jenny seems to have misunderstood what being the customer's advocate means. In this situation it's unlikely her organization wants to make a pricing exception for one customer. Jenny needs to represent her organization as well as her customers. If you checked 1, 2, 3, and 5, we are in agreement.

ELEMENT 5: Take Responsibility

Who is responsible for your behavior and performance at work? The answer is simple–you! The following is a list of many of your responsibilities. See if you agree. You can probably add a few of your own.

I am responsible for the following:

- ❑ Extending courtesy toward customers
- ❑ Extending courtesy toward co-workers
- ❑ Acting with civility at all times
- ❑ Maintaining high ethical behavior and standards
- ❑ Accepting others
- ❑ Maintaining a positive attitude
- ❑ Being sensitive toward co-workers' feelings and needs
- ❑ Promoting teamwork and call center success
- ❑ Acceptable grooming and personal care including appropriate dress
- ❑ Continually striving for improved job performance
- ❑ Using the tools and training provided
- ❑ Using good judgment
- ❑ Making effective decisions
- ❑ Minimizing office drama and gossip
- ❑ ______________________________
- ❑ ______________________________
- ❑ ______________________________

Successful CSRs practice all these behaviors. If your organization doesn't encourage these behaviors, take it upon yourself to promote them and lead by example. You will be surprised at how quickly your positive behavior will impact those around you.

Using Good Judgment

Acting responsibly requires using good judgment in the many decisions you will make throughout the day. Your own good judgment will help you make the best choices about how to interact with others, both customers and co-workers.

Building Trust

By hiring you, the call center has already placed a certain amount of trust in you–trust that you can learn new skills, trust that you will represent the organization in a positive way, and trust that you will do your best every day. When you demonstrate that you are capable of making good choices, management will place an even higher level of trust in you–they will trust you to make decisions on how to best meet customers' needs. The extent of this trust will vary, depending on the flexibility of the organization's policies and procedures, on the type of products and services you offer, and on the nature of the customers' requests.

Showing Initiative

Each action you take tells management a little bit more about how much trust they can place in you. Some CSRs mistakenly think that they are showing good judgment by asking for permission before making any decisions. In the busy call center environment, your supervisor cannot be expected to "hold your hand" at every moment. The professional CSR asks questions when information is not otherwise available, but then stores that information and puts it to use when faced with a similar situation in the future. This is called taking initiative, an essential skill for the professional CSR.

By the same token, reps must use good judgment in knowing when it is appropriate to involve management in a decision. Some decisions are simply too important to make without some input and guidance from others.

Acting Empowered

In its simplest form, empowerment means the CSR can respond to the customer's needs without first getting management's approval. In the enlightened organization, the rep is expected to act empowered, and minor conflicts over good judgment are expected. But, working together toward customer satisfaction remains the primary goal.

You Make the Decision

Mr. Anderson wanted a refund of his membership fee because he had not used the services Mark's company offered. Mark explained that there is no refund policy. Mr. Anderson explained that he had been in the hospital for several weeks and couldn't use the services. Mark decided he would see if he could get Mr. Anderson an extension. Mark met with his supervisor and they had a short meeting with the call center manager. Mark pleaded his case. He said Mr. Anderson is a long-time customer who has been unable to use the services because of illness and, out of fairness, his membership services should be extended. Mark asked for a 60-day extension. The manager and supervisor decided they could offer 30 days. Mark called Mr. Anderson and told him about the extension. Mr. Anderson thought the extension should have been longer, but overall he said he was satisfied.

What do you think of Mark's performance? Did he balance the customer's need with his company's interest? Do you think Mark used good judgment? Did he act empowered?

Compare Mark's performance with Jenny's performance on page 17. Circle the name you think answers the questions best.

Who used better judgment?	**Mark or Jenny**
Who provided better customer service?	**Mark or Jenny**
Who was the better customer advocate?	**Mark or Jenny**
Who represented their organization better?	**Mark or Jenny**
Who needs to better understand empowerment?	**Mark or Jenny**

Mark's name should be circled in all places.

ELEMENT 6: Make a Commitment

Being committed to your call center job doesn't mean you have decided to work there for the rest of your working life, but it does require you to be professional and provide quality customer service. To be successful, you will need to commit to learning and using your communication skills. Developing professionalism and learning quality customer service skills will benefit you in all areas of your life. These skills will help you be more successful in any career you choose and they will also help you communicate better in your personal life.

Defining commitment is difficult, but some of the qualities include striving to do your best, meeting job responsibilities, and taking advantage of learning opportunities. Commitment also means demonstrating a desire to work with and help other members of the call center team.

Call center teamwork is different from "traditional" teamwork. In the call center, teamwork focuses on sharing.

What needs to be shared?

- **Your positive attitude.** Make certain it rubs off on others.
- **Information.** New policies, changes, promotions, and updates need to be communicated.
- **Ideas on call management.**
- **Your leadership.** Set a good example.

What should *not* be shared?

- Office gossip and drama.
- Complaints about customers and other work-related incidences.

So make a commitment to sharing those things that will help make the entire team successful. And make a commitment to setting a good example by acting professionally, taking initiative, and giving your customers the best possible service every day.

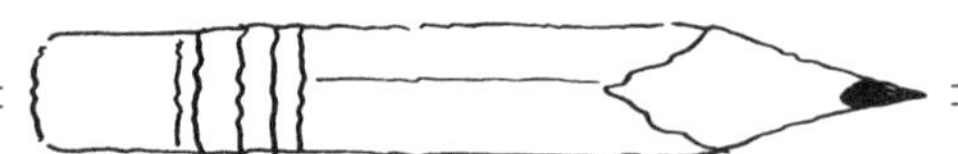

Rate Your Level of Commitment

Rate your level of commitment on these topics. Then rate your co-workers. Finally, rate how you feel your co-workers see you.

1 = Poor 2 = Fair 3 = Average 4 = Good 5 = Excellent

Topic	How I rate myself	How I rate my co-workers	How my co-workers would rate me
Am I a team player?	______	______	______
Do I take initiative in trying to satisfy my customers?	______	______	______
How good is my judgment?	______	______	______
Do I avoid gossip and drama?	______	______	______
Do I share my positive attitude?	______	______	______
How well do I set a good example?	______	______	______

We tend to rate our efforts higher than the ratings we give our co-workers. For an interesting learning experience take this exercise into a work unit meeting and share your ratings with your co-workers.

PART 3

The All-Important Customer

Recognizing the Customer's Style

Understanding customer behavior is another important key to being a successful CSR. Each customer is different, and each has a unique behavioral style. Accurately recognizing and responding to customer's style increases customer satisfaction. Here's an example.

Carmel received several calls from customers who had not received their orders. She knew that shipping was swamped with orders and had also experienced computer problems. She was careful not to mention the computer problems to the customers. Mrs. Davis called and asked about her order. She said; "I placed my order on the 7th, and I was promised a delivery date of the 15th. It's now the 17th and I haven't received my order." Carmel explained to Mrs. Davis that orders were running three days behind and that her order would arrive the next day, the 18th. Carmel also apologized for the delay. Mrs. Davis wasn't satisfied. She asked; "What caused the delay?" Carmel explained that her company had been swamped with orders. Mrs. Davis wanted to know why. Carmel explained that demand was very high for their products. Mrs. Davis seemed satisfied with the explanation. Carmel's next call was from Mr. Winters. Mr. Winters wanted to know where his order was. Carmel explained the shipping delay and that his order would arrive on the 13th. Mr. Winters said thank you and he hung up. These two customers had the same need, but they required different responses to be satisfied.

Carmel spent more time with Mrs. Davis than she did with Mr. Winters. Mrs. Davis' behavior is referred to as analytical while Mr. Winter's behavior is assertive. CSRs need to recognize these different customer behaviors and know how to respond to each.

Everyone is unique and no two customers will behave exactly the same way. Most people will exhibit a blend of behavioral styles depending on the situation or under varying circumstances. But most people tend toward one behavioral style a majority of the time. Learning to recognize the characteristics of each style will help prepare you to respond in the most effective way for each customer.

The Analytical Customer

Analytical customers are sometimes called thinkers or detail-oriented. This type of customer is motivated by accuracy. Mrs. Davis, in our example, wasn't satisfied knowing her order would arrive the next day; she wanted details on why it was delayed.

Characteristics of the Analytical Customer

- Needs a lot of information to make a decision
- Wants to work with facts and figures more than with people
- Is focused on the business side of things not the social or relationship side
- Tends to be quiet and more introspective
- Is a good listener
- Doesn't like to be rushed
- Prefers an organized approach to things
- Is patient
- Is not very direct or assertive
- May seem abrupt at times
- Uses a slower more careful rate of speech than an assertive person

The Assertive Customer

Assertive customers are often called drivers or directors. As an assertive personality, Mr. Winters is result-oriented and details are of less importance to him. Assertive customers are motivated by action and results and are difficult for most reps to manage. These customers are so assertive and direct with their requests and statements that reps sometimes think they are angry.

Characteristics of the Assertive Customer

- Wants and usually demands action
- Is very direct and to the point in their statements
- Makes it clear what they want
- Has a lack of patience
- Uses a faster rate of speech
- Is quick to make decisions
- Seems rude at times
- Focuses on results not on relationships
- Wants answers now!
- Usually not interested in the details
- They are not angry, just being assertive

Tailoring Your Responses

To better understand these analytical and assertive behaviors, look at some effective responses for these customers.

SITUATION 1: Customer has not received her refund check

CSR responding to an analytical customer:

> *"I understand why you feel that way. There are three things I'll do for you. First I'll find out why the check wasn't sent. Next, I'll verify the amount, and finally, if the check has not been mailed, I'll follow up to make certain the check goes out by Friday. Will that be acceptable?"*

Note how the CSR explained the details of his action plan. Look at the same situation except the customer is assertive.

CSR responding to an assertive customer:

> *"I'm sorry this happened. Your check will be issued on Friday, and you should receive it the following week. Will that be acceptable?"*

The CSR was direct and to the point.

SITUATION 2: Customer called and placed a small order

CSR responding to an analytical customer:

> *"Shall I review your order for you?"*

Knowing the analytical customer wants assurance, the order was taken down accurately, the CSR offers to review the order.

CSR responding to an assertive customer:

> *"Thanks for your order. Is there anything else I can help you with?"*

With an assertive person who probably doesn't want to spend time reviewing the order, the CSR is direct.

Guidelines for Analytical and Assertive Customers

In our examples the response to the analytical customer always provided more detail and explanation. The response to the assertive customer was more direct and to the point. As you learn to recognize these different behaviors it becomes easier to respond appropriately. Use the following guidelines to help you satisfy these different–and sometimes difficult–customers.

When talking with the Analytical Customer:

- ➤ Be very accurate
- ➤ Discuss the relevant details of the situation
- ➤ Don't rush
- ➤ Remember this customer needs time to think before making a decision
- ➤ Present your services in logical and concise terms
- ➤ Answer questions with appropriate details
- ➤ Don't expect much social conversation
- ➤ If you are assertive, slow down a little
- ➤ Listen to their needs

When talking to the Assertive Customer:

- ➤ Keep in mind the assertive customer wants action and results
- ➤ You may have to pick up the pace of the conversation
- ➤ Provide only details that are essential
- ➤ Don't mistake the assertiveness you hear for anger
- ➤ Be direct and get to the point
- ➤ Don't expect much social conversation
- ➤ Don't be offended by the abruptness you hear, remember that they are more interested in efficiency than personal pleasantries

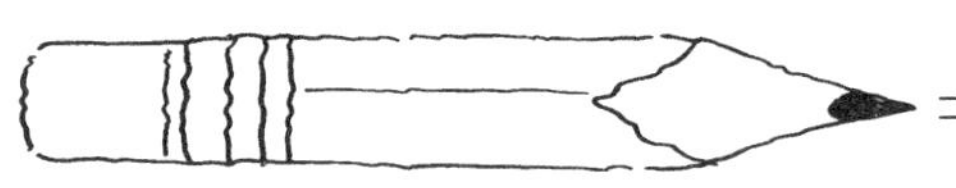

Recognizing Behavioral Styles

A. Determine if an analytical or assertive customer made each statement or question below. Check (✔) the corresponding box.

Analytical	Assertive	
❑	❑	1. I'm not interested in all that. When will I get it?
❑	❑	2. I don't understand. When I called in on the 9th the rep said I could use the coupon anytime. Now you are telling me there's a limitation. I'll need an explanation of what's going on here.
❑	❑	3. I'll have to think about this. Can you send a technical manual?
❑	❑	4. There are four things we need to discuss. Let me describe them.
❑	❑	5. No, and that's final.
❑	❑	6. I need an answer now.
❑	❑	7. I don't understand why it takes so long to get an answer.
❑	❑	8. I'll have to talk to your supervisor about this.
❑	❑	9. Put your supervisor on the phone.
❑	❑	10. Angry? I'm not angry I just want you to do something about this mess.

Bonus questions:

B. Write down two characteristics that are common to both the analytical and assertive customers.

____

____

C. Analytical customers are motivated by:

____

D. Assertive customers are motivated by:

____

How good are you at recognizing Analytic and Assertive behavioral styles? Compare your answers to the Answer Key on page 38.

Understanding Your Own Behavioral Style

Like customers and other callers, you have a distinct behavioral style, too. Perhaps you typically display assertive or analytical behavior. How does this affect your relationship with customers?

If you're typically assertive you need to:

- Slow down a little during conversations
- Give the customer time to think
- Slow your rate of speech when necessary
- Force yourself to listen closely
- Let the customer talk

As an assertive person, you are motivated by immediate action. Unless your customer is also assertive he or she will be less focused on action and more interested in accuracy, exchanging pleasantries, details, and discussing your products or services. You have to modify your behavior to satisfy the customer.

If you're analytical you need to:

- Pick up your pace during conversations
- Realize that many customers are not detail-oriented

As an analytical person, you are focused on accuracy. Your customer may want action and some social conversation. To satisfy the customer, you will have to modify your behavior.

Eight Customer Needs

When customers rely on you to answer questions, resolve problems, provide products, or otherwise meet their needs, they have some specific expectations. Customers want the following when working with a CSR:

- Fast service
- Courteous service
- Consistent service
- Someone who will listen
- A knowledgeable rep
- Expert advice
- Smooth transactions
- A commitment

Need 1: Fast Service

When customers are on hold for long periods of time, they can become impatient. Your job is to recognize the customer has been waiting and when appropriate apologize for the wait. Simply saying, "I'm sorry you had to wait so long" often calms a customer. Now that the customer is in your capable hands, it's up to you to provide the fast service she wants. When service is slowed for any reason, you should give a general apology.

"I'm sorry about this delay," or

"I know you expected faster service. Please accept my apologies."

Need 2: Courteous Service

Customers want to be treated with civility, which means using an expected, acceptable code of behavior that includes politeness and courtesy. Being civil and treating the customer with respect, minimizes potential conflicts.

Civil language sounds like this:

"Thank you."

"You're welcome."

"How may I help you?"

"Thanks for calling."

"We appreciate your business."

Other key words are: *please*, *you*, *may I*, *if you please*, and *if you don't mind.*

Need 3: Consistent Service

Every time customers call the call center, they expect to receive a high level of service. Sometimes customers say, "The level of service depends on who I get when I call." Consistent service means the customer can depend on a high level of service every time he calls.

Need 4: Someone Who Will Listen

Customers expect you to listen to their needs. They don't want to repeat their requests or explanations, and they don't like errors. If you fail to listen closely and you provide the wrong information, you have created a problem and possibly an irate customer.

Need 5: A Knowledgeable Rep

Customers expect excellent product and service knowledge. They don't want call backs or other delays. They want to make their inquiry and get an immediate and accurate response.

Need 6: Expert Advice

Often customers want and need suggestions. Perhaps there are two or more options and each has its benefits. The customer isn't sure what to do, so you make a suggestion based on your experience. The customer agrees and is satisfied. Here's an example.

Offering Advice

Whenever customers hesitate or sound as if they are looking for advice, offer to help. If you are in doubt as to what the customer wants, simply ask; "May I make a suggestion?" or "Would you like my advice?" Customers will generally be grateful for your assistance. Remember, you're the expert on your products and services.

Michelle's company offered three warranties. Mrs. Lofton said she wanted a warranty, but she was undecided which one suited her needs best. Michelle explained the benefits of each warranty, including the associated costs. Mrs. Lofton was still hesitant. Michelle then asked Mrs. Lofton a few questions about her situation. Michelle quickly determined which warranty Mrs. Lofton should purchase. She said, "Mrs. Lofton, based on what you have told me the 36-month warranty is the best choice for you. It offers the highest cost savings for your situation. " Michelle went on to explain the savings. Mrs. Lofton purchased the 36-month warranty.

Don't let the customer make a bad decision. Providing the customer with the best service is always the best choice.

Need 7: Smooth Transactions

The experienced rep knows how to make the complex look simple. Organizations sometimes mistakenly place obstacles in front of the customer. When this happens, the rep has to smooth things over with the customer. Experienced CSRs know how to make new policies work for the customer.

> *"Don't worry. It's not that confusing. Let me explain it for you."*
>
> *"I can quickly show you how the new policy will help you."*
>
> *"I understand why you don't like the changes. Perhaps we can go over them together and I can point out some of the benefits."*

It is the CSR's responsibility to make things go as smoothly as possible for the customer. CSRs can make things go more smoothly by taking a few extra moments to explain something to a customer. A rep may also alert management to problems with new policies or other changes.

Need 8: A Specific Commitment

When customers have a problem or an issue that needs resolution, they want a commitment for when they can expect an answer. Too often customers hear, "I'll get back to you on this," or "I'll have someone call you," or "Let me look into it, and I'll call you back." Customers want you to make a specific commitment and follow through on it.

> *"Let me look into your billing question. I can call you this afternoon around four o'clock. Is that a good time to call?"*
>
> *"I'll talk to our sales group and determine what happened. It will take a couple of days. I can call you on Friday morning. Is that a good time to call?"*
>
> *"I'm sorry I don't have an answer for you at the moment. Let me look into this, and I'll call you back later in the week. What would be a good time for me to call?"*

Those are eight common customer needs. Can you think of others?

____

____

____

____

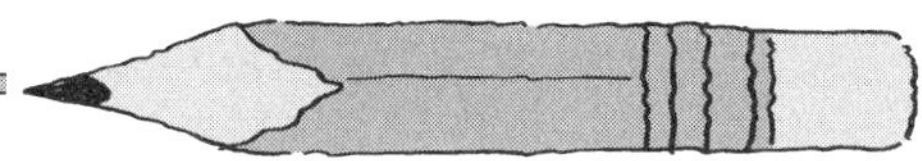

Answer Key: Recognizing Behavioral Styles

Analytical	Assertive	
❑	☑	1. I'm not interested in all that. When will I get it?
☑	❑	2. I don't understand. When I called in on the 9th the rep said I could use the coupon anytime. Now you are telling me there's a limitation. I'll need an explanation of what's going on here.
☑	❑	3. I'll have to think about this. Can you send a technical manual?
☑	❑	4. There are four things we need to discuss. Let me describe them.
❑	☑	5. No, and that's final.
❑	☑	6. I need an answer now.
☑	❑	7. I don't understand why it takes so long to get an answer.
❑	☑	8. I'll have to talk to your supervisor about this.
❑	☑	9. Put your supervisor on the phone.
❑	☑	10. Angry? I'm not angry I just want you to do something about this mess.

Bonus questions:

B. *little social conversation, and focused on business rather than relationships*

C. *accuracy*

D. *action and results*

P A R T **4**

Building Your Communication Skills

Ten Essential Communication Skills

Total customer satisfaction is determined by a variety of factors, but none is more important than the customer's experience with the call center. That contact must be managed in a professional manner, and the CSR must draw on a set of customer satisfying skills.

Professional reps have a set of communication skills that they can apply to any customer situation. They are so adept and well-versed in using these skills that they can quickly call upon the right skill at the right time for the right situation.

These essential communication skills will help you:

- Know what to say and what not to say
- Remain calm
- Be positive
- Stay ready for the next call

Learning the following skills will strengthen your ability to provide a high level of customer service:

1. **Listening Effectively**
2. **Extending Common Courtesy**
3. **Avoiding the Wrong Impression**
4. **Using the Customer's Language**
5. **Gathering Customer Information**
6. **Satisfying the Angry Customer**
7. **Managing Technology**
8. **Writing Effective Email**
9. **Preparing a Mental Script**
10. **Closing the Conversation**

SKILL 1: Listening Effectively

Customers want you to listen closely and understand their needs. Your ability to listen plays a key role in your success with customers, co-workers, and management.

Petra began the performance review meeting with Eric by praising his ability to manage a large volume of calls. She said the only area of concern was the accuracy on many of Eric's orders, which had caused customer complaints. Eric said he was concerned as well. Petra asked if Eric understood the new order entry system. Eric replied that he was very comfortable with it. After further discussion, Petra asked Eric to think about how well he was listening to customers. Eric agreed that might be the problem because he felt rushed most of the time. "It seems like I'm rushing through one customer call to get to the next one," he said. Petra replied, "Rushing might be keeping you from hearing exactly what the customer says."

Improving your listening skills begins with a self-appraisal. Take an honest look at your listening habits and then rate yourself.

Rate Your Listening Skills

On a scale of 1 to 10, how do you rate your ability to hear and listen to the customer?

1 = Poor 5 = Average 10 = Excellent

1 2 3 4 5 6 7 8 9 10

Most of us have room for improvement when it comes to listening. Following are a few ideas on how to improve your listening.

Hearing What the Customer Wants

Customers hate being asked the same question more than once. Unfortunately it's all too typical. It usually goes like this:

Rep: *Good morning, technical support. How may I help you?*

Customer: *This is Bob Randolph calling. I downloaded the specs on your laser printer but I have some questions.*

Rep: *Did you purchase one of our laser printers?*

Customer: *No, not yet, I'm thinking about buying one.*

Rep: *Our website covers our laser printers in considerable detail. Did you take a look at it?*

Customer: *That's where I downloaded the specs from.*

Rep: *Oh. How can I help you?*

Customer: *I have some questions regarding your printer's graphics capability, and I need more information on your rebate.*

Rep: *I think you need to talk with sales. I'll transfer you. May I have your name?*

Customer: *Bob Randolph. Why can't you help me?*

Rep: *I only deal with technical matters and questions. Salespeople handle questions regarding rebates and pricing.*

Customer: *I have questions regarding the printer's graphics capability.*

Rep: *Oh. I didn't understand that. First, can I get your customer number?*

Customer: *I don't have a customer number. I haven't purchase anything yet. I just have a few questions about the printer's graphics capability. I feel like I'm going in circles here!*

Rep: *Oh, I'm sorry. What questions do you have?*

This potential customer is well on his way to frustration because tech support isn't listening carefully. How much more of this run around do you think it would take before Mr. Randolph got really angry? Most customers don't complain when confronted with this type of frustration; instead, they find someone else to do business with.

Often there are obstacles to overcome before you can hear and understand what the customer wants. Where do those obstacles come from? You often create them yourself, without even realizing it.

Can You Repeat That?

Asking a customer to repeat what was said previously should occur as infrequently as possible. But when you do forget important information, there is a way to handle it. In our previous examples, the CSRs politely asked the customer for their names, but they did not acknowledge that the customer had already provided their names. They should have said something like:

> *"I'm sorry, but may I have your name again?"*
>
> *"Would you spell your last name for me?" (if this will work)*
>
> *"Would you mind giving me your name again?"*

When you have to ask about other previously provided information, use the same approach.

> *"I'm sorry, I didn't get all of your account number. Would you please repeat it?"*
>
> *"My apologies, but would you please give me your customer number again?"*
>
> *"Excuse me, but I didn't understand all of that. Would you mind repeating what you said?"*

How frequently do you find yourself asking customers to repeat themselves? If you need to decrease these requests, start writing down information as the customer provides it. Your goal is to ask customers to repeat information infrequently or not at all.

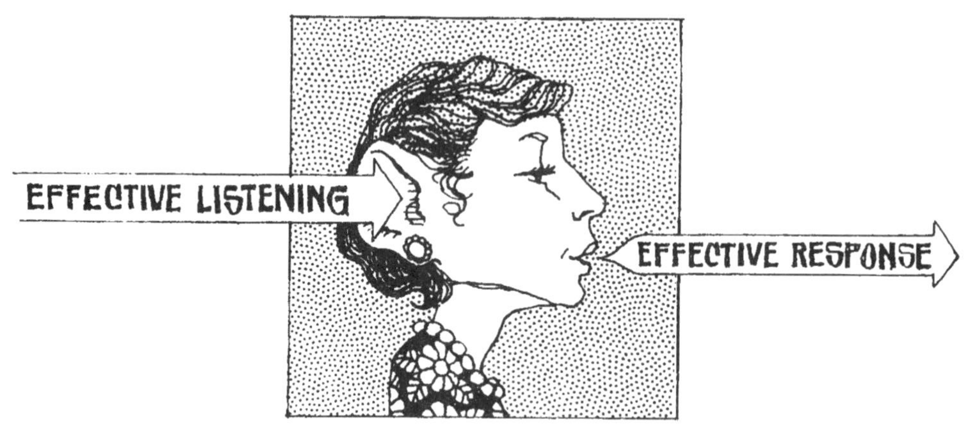

Listening Is an Important Part of Communicating

Picture a co-worker you consider a "strong communicator." Most likely, this person is articulate, forceful, entertaining at times, and has a good command of language. This person is probably a good listener. Being a good listener is an important part of your overall ability to communicate.

Effective listening begins with understanding what the customer wants:

➤ Hear the reason for the customer's call

➤ Focus on what the customer has to say

➤ Listen for what the customer is interested in

Often there are obstacles to overcome before you can hear and understand what the customer wants. Where do those obstacles come from? You often create them yourself, without even realizing it.

Overcoming Listening Obstacles

The following is a list of potential obstacles to listening. Check (✔) those that apply to you. At the bottom of the list add any other personal listening obstacles you can think of.

Obstacles to effective listening:

- ❑ Hearing what you want to hear
- ❑ Thinking of what you are going to say next
- ❑ Distractions such as co-workers, noise, side conversations, etc.
- ❑ Thinking about the previous customer call
- ❑ Worrying about the next customer call or work in general
- ❑ Stress
- ❑ Difficulty in understanding what the customer says
- ❑ Getting involved emotionally (instead of logically) in the customer conversation
- ❑ Misreading the customer's behavioral style
- ❑ Talking too much or talking when you should be listening
- ❑ Holding preconceived ideas about the customer's inquiry
- ❑ Thinking about personal issues
- ❑ Boredom
- ❑ Making assumptions rather asking questions
- ❑ Others:

____

____

____

Being aware of obstacles that negatively impact your listening can help you eliminate these roadblocks or substantially reduce their impact.

Defining Your Communication Style

Just as your customers (and everyone else) have a dominant behavioral style, you also have a definable communication style. Your style is reflected in how you speak and how you listen. Once you understand your communication preference, you can modify it to satisfy customers who have a different style.

FOUR TYPES OF COMMUNICATION STYLES

Amiable

Amiable people tend to be people-oriented and enjoy helping customers. These types are patient, but sometimes too patient because their calls tend to be long. CSRs who are amiable are good listeners, and they seldom have to ask customers to repeat themselves. Amiable types believe that working together is the best way to solve problems and answer questions.

Analytical

Analytical people are thorough and strive to be accurate. They don't like to be rushed. These analytical types believe the details, facts, and figures are important to know and discuss.

Driver

Drivers tend to be assertive and enjoy a fast pace. Their favorite calls are short and to the point without much social interaction. A driver determines customer needs quickly and takes appropriate action. During slow-paced customer conversations, drivers tend to become impatient.

Outgoing

Outgoing types like a faster pace. They like to talk and have some fun during calls. When there are a lot of details or the conversation slows, outgoing people get bored. Customers generally like outgoing CSRs and enjoy talking with them.

Adapting to Your Customer's Style

Which communication style is the best? They are all equal. But it is important to modify your style to satisfy the customer. Here are some general guidelines that will help.

For Amiable Customers...

Amiable customers are a little easier to satisfy, but they have unique needs as well. They generally believe that working together is the best approach.

- ➤ Listen for their need to build a relationship with you–respond in kind
- ➤ Demonstrate your patience as a listener
- ➤ Listen to their social conversation
- ➤ If you are assertive or outgoing, slow your conversational pace
- ➤ Listen for opportunities to move the conversation forward

For Analytical Customers...

What if the customer is analytical? This customer has a slower pace and wants time to think. They are looking for accuracy and details. For these customers, you can:

- ➤ Slow down and carefully listen, especially if you tend to be assertive or outgoing
- ➤ Focus on accuracy and listen carefully for important details
- ➤ Provide time for the analytical to think and decide
- ➤ Listen to their "accurate and thorough" explanations
- ➤ Listen to see if they are completely satisfied with your response
- ➤ When in doubt ask
- ➤ Be a patient listener

For Drivers or Outgoing Customers...

If you are speaking with a customer who talks a little fast, makes very direct statements, and seems to want an immediate answer or solution, you are probably listening to an assertive or outgoing customer. To satisfy these customers:

- ➤ Listen for and then match some of their conversational pace
- ➤ Listen closely to their need and respond with directness
- ➤ Listen for an opportunity to present your solution or an action plan
- ➤ Don't "hear" the assertive customer's directness as abruptness
- ➤ If they are more outgoing and talkative, let them talk while you listen

As you listen to your customers, try to identify their styles within the first few moments of the conversation. After a little practice, you will be able to recognize the different styles readily.

SKILL 2: Extending Common Courtesy

The language of common courtesy needs to be woven into your dialogue with all customers. Many phrases and words are used to convey common courtesy. One of the most powerful phrases is *thank you.*

"Thank you for calling."

"Thanks for your business."

"Thank you for being so patient."

"Thanks for holding."

"Thank you for choosing us."

Two more powerful common courtesy phrases are *may I* and *please.*

"May I please have your account number?"

"May I have your name?"

"May I please have your shipping address?"

"Please call us anytime you have questions."

"Will you please call me if there are any further problems?"

"May I put you on hold for a moment?"

You can use one or more of these statements on every customer call. Customers, like the rest of us, want to be appreciated, and these phrases let customers know how important they are.

The Most Powerful Courtesy: The Customer's Name

Experienced reps say the most powerful courtesy words are the customer's name. The theory is that customers like to hear their names. Using the customer's name is important, but be careful not to over use it. A conversation with too much emphasis on the name can be overkill and distracting. Here are some examples.

Overkill

Rep: *Mrs. Sinclair, I really appreciate you calling. Your March bill, Mrs. Sinclair, has a balance due of $99.09. Mrs. Sinclair, we would appreciate your prompt attention to this balance. Mrs. Sinclair, when do you think that you will be able to make the payment?*

Speaking of customer names, a long-standing question in customer service is: *When do I address a customer by her first name?* You should address customers by their first names only if they ask you to.

Overly Familiar

Customer: *My name is Morgan Street, and I have some questions regarding your membership offer.*

Rep: *Thanks for calling, Morgan. I'll be glad to help you.*

Respectful

Customer: *My name is Morgan Street, and I have some questions regarding your membership offer.*

Rep: *Thanks for calling, Ms. Street. I'll be glad to help you.*

Using titles such as Ms., Mrs., and Mr. shows respect.

Practicing Courtesy

List all the different ways you can frame a basic question using common courtesy.

When you need the customer's name, how can you best ask this question? Write your responses here.

____

____

____

When you have forgotten the customer's name how can you best pose the question "What is your name?"

____

____

____

When you need the customer's address, how can you best ask for it?

____

____

____

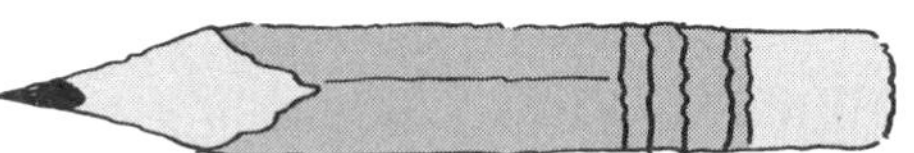

Answer Key: Practice Courtesy

Answers will vary, but they should be along these lines.

When you need the customer's name, how can you best ask this question? Write your responses here.

May I have your name?

May I have your name please?

May I please have your name?

When you have forgotten the customer's name how can you best pose the question "What is your name?"

I'm sorry, may I please have your name again?

Would you please spell your last name for me?

I'm sorry, would you repeat your name for me?

When you need the customer's address, how can you best ask for it?

May I have your address, including your zip?

Please give me your address and zip code.

I'll need your address please.

Courteous Conversations in Action

Here are two examples of conversations where a customer is calling to place an order for picture framing material. The customer has ordered from this company previously.

Example 1

Rep: *Graphics Quick Frames. This is Liz, how may I help you?*

Customer: *I need to order some frames.*

Rep: *What is the number on the catalog you are looking at?*

Customer: *Where do I find the number?*

Rep: *On the back cover.*

Customer: *It's P99QF01.*

Rep: *Have your ordered from us before?*

Customer: *Yes.*

Rep: *Do you have your customer number?*

Customer: *I have the invoice in front of me. Where is the customer number?*

Rep: *At the top of the invoice.*

Customer: *I don't see it…here it is…970464.*

Rep: *What would you like to order?*

The rep verified the customer's name and address, but she failed to use any courtesy words. The conversation lacks civility.

The customer placed the order and the rep entered the information. A question came up about papermat color.

Customer: *I want to match a color called script white. Can you tell which one of your whites would be the closest to script white?*

Rep: *I have no way to do that.*

Customer: *Okay, I'll take arctic white then.*

The customer and the rep discussed a few other details of the order in the same manner, and then the rep said,

Rep: *What is your credit card number?*

The customer gave the number and expiration date and heard nothing until a few moments later.

Rep: *Your order comes to $154.00.*

Customer: *Okay.*

Rep: *Thanks for calling Graphics Quick Frames.*

Example 2

Here's how the conversation should have gone. See if you agree.

Rep: *Good morning, Graphics Quick Frames, this is Liz. How may I help you?*

Customer: *I need to order some frames.*

Rep: *Have you ordered from us before?*

Customer: *Yes.*

Rep: *Good. Do you know your customer number? If you have your previous invoice the number will be in top right-hand corner.*

Customer: *I have it right here. The number is 970464.*

Rep: *Thank you. If you don't mind, would you please give me the number of the catalog you're using? The number is on the back page on the lower right-hand side.*

Customer: *It's P99QF01.*

Rep: *Thank you. What would you like to order?*

As before, the rep enters the information.

Customer: *I want to match a color called script white. Is there any way you could tell which one of your whites would be the closest?*

Rep: *What we can do, if you have the time, is send me a small piece of your script white papermat and I can try to match it to one of our whites. Would you like to do that?*

Customer: *Not this time. But when I have more time, I might do that.*

Rep: *Keep in mind that we'll be glad to help you match the color. I'm sure we can get pretty close.*

Customer: *Okay. Thank you.*

The customer and the rep discuss the final details of the order, and then the rep says:

Rep: *May I please have your credit card number, the expiration date, and your name as it appears on the card?*

The customer provides the information.

Rep: *Thank you. Your total comes to $154.00.*

Customer: *Okay.*

Rep: *Is there anything else I can help you with?*

Customer: *No.*

Rep: *Thanks for calling Mr. Haynes. We appreciate your business.*

Which conversation do you think leaves a more positive impression? Note the difference between the conversations. One is cold and matter-of-fact while the other includes civility.

Special Opportunities

Special opportunities are excellent times to extend courtesy toward customers. Here are four examples of times when using courtesy will have an exceptionally positive impact on the customer.

OPPORTUNITY 1: The customer has made an error

An obnoxious customer calls and describes how messed up your organization is because you didn't "do this or that." You get this guy to calm down a little so you can check out the situation. Surprise! You learn the customer's error caused the problem. Next, you explain to the customer what happened. The customer apologizes sheepishly and says he feels terrible. What do you do? You let the customer off by extending courtesy. You might say:

"Please don't worry about it. These things happen."

"I'm glad we solved the problem. I am not concerned about what caused it."

"We appreciate your business, and I'm happy we found the problem."

"This sort of thing happens occasionally. Don't worry about it. It's all taken care of now."

Most customers will remember your courtesy for a long time.

OPPORTUNITY 2: The angry customer

One of the *musts* of talking with an irate customer is to remain courteous. When the customer is angry and discourteous, you should not reply in kind. Experienced CSRs have learned that most angry customers will calm down once they have expressed their problem, and they realize you are going to help them. Courteous responses sound like:

"I'm sorry this happened."

"I'm sorry that you are upset."

"I completely understand, and I'm sorry about this situation but let's do this…"

"I don't blame you for feeling upset."

"I'm very sorry about this. Please tell me what you would like me to do?"

OPPORTUNITY 3: The understanding customer

Usually, customers are nice people. When they are especially understanding and patient, they deserve extra courtesy. Suppose, for whatever reason, you struggled providing what the customer needed. The customer experienced delays, long hold times, and a little confusion, yet the customer was always patient and understanding. The customer's understanding deserves recognition. Whenever a customer has been inconvenienced, you should be extra courteous.

> *"I really appreciate your patience."*
>
> *"I'm sorry this took so long. Thanks for being so understanding."*
>
> *"Thanks for your understanding."*
>
> *"I'm sorry you had to hold so long."*
>
> *"I'm sorry the shipment was late."*
>
> *"Please accept my apologies for the delay."*

We tend to postpone responding to the understanding customer because we are more concerned with the demanding customer. Here's an example.

> *Miguel had three customers to email. First, he responded to Joe, who was angry over a previous call. Next, he emailed Sonja Powerful, a very assertive customer. Miguel didn't have time to email Norman Niceguy so he decided to delay that email until the next morning.*

The understanding customer deserves your attention. The patient nice customer may change behavior if there is too much service delay. They, too, can become assertive and demanding.

OPPORTUNITY 4: The customer you can't help

Sometimes you simply can't help a customer. The customer needs a service you don't provide or is making demands you can't meet. In this situation, your response needs to be courteous.

"I'm sorry Mr. Jones, but we've done all that we can."

"Please try and understand our position. I'm sorry but we simply do not offer that service."

"I wish I could help you."

"Please understand, I would like to help but…"

"I understand your request but I'm sorry we can't…"

In this situation the call may end without the customer being completely satisfied. These situations are unfortunate, but the customer did receive courteous treatment and that is always important.

SKILL 3: Avoiding Statements That Give the Wrong Impression

As you move about the call center, do you occasionally hear inappropriate statements made to customers? Everything said to a customer leaves an impression. To leave a positive impression, you must provide quality service and phrase your responses positively.

Keep Negative Organization Information to Yourself

Do not share organizational problems with the customer. Nearly every call center experiences occasional increases in customer hold times, periods of understaffing, new product introductions that don't go smoothly, and countless other problems. In time the problems are solved and everything gets back to normal. Discuss the problems with co-workers but leave the customer out of the process.

Don't Be Critical of Other Work Units

If you work with other groups (shipping, accounting, tech support, sales) don't criticize these work units. The customer doesn't need to hear that shipping is backed up and there are delays, that sales misquoted the new pricing to a few hundred customers, that tech support training is way behind schedule, or that your marketing people haven't made things very clear. Most of us are bothered occasionally by something about our organization. Don't involve the customer in your gripes through a slip of the tongue or a critical statement.

Customers don't need to hear critical statements about individual co-workers either. If a customer criticizes a co-worker, it is best to not acknowledge the criticism, or if appropriate, respond with a positive statement.

Keep Your Remarks Positive

Standard, everyday responses can be changed to be more positive. Suppose your customers are experiencing long hold times.

When the customer complains, what do you say?

> *"I'm sorry about the wait but we are swamped with calls."*

Or, do you make it positive?

> *"I'm sorry about the delay, but the demand for our service has been very high."*

Have you overheard statements like these?

> "I don't think he knew what he was doing."
>
> "She's new and doesn't know very much."
>
> "He's from accounting, and they never want to help customers."
>
> "I'm sorry she couldn't help, but she rarely does."
>
> "I'm sorry about the delay. I don't know why they can't answer their phones."
>
> "Looks like we messed up again."
>
> "The new pricing seems high, doesn't it?"
>
> "I know, the call delays are getting worse by the day."
>
> "You're not the only customer upset by this change."
>
> "We just don't seem to be able to get your account straightened out."
>
> "I'd ask my supervisor, but he doesn't know anything."

Here are a few other examples of less than positive statements.

Situation: *The customer has been on hold for a long time.*

Rep: *"I'm sorry about the long wait, but we are understaffed today."*

Situation: *The customer is upset about a late charge.*

Rep: *"I understand how you must feel. Many customers have been upset over our new policy regarding late charges."*

Situation: *The customer needs a technical explanation.*

Rep: *"I'm sorry, I can't answer all your questions. We haven't been trained yet."*

Situation: *The customer has been transferred to the call center by mistake.*

Rep: *"I don't know why tech support transferred you to me. They are always doing something stupid."*

Here are a few examples of how statements can be rephrased to be more positive.

Typical Statement: *"I think we'll be able to help you."*

Improved Statement: *"I'll be glad to help you."*

Typical Statement: *"I'll try and have someone call you this afternoon."*

Improved Statement: *"I'll have someone call you before three o'clock."*

In each improved statement only a slight change was necessary to make it a more positive response.

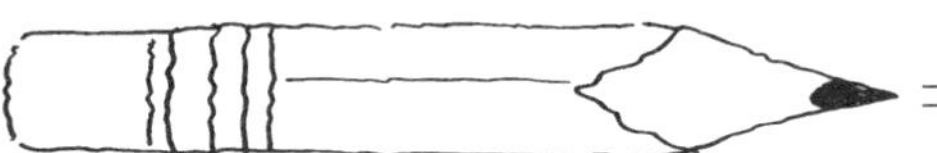

Creating Positive Statements

Most reps repeat the same information and statements throughout the day. Make a list of three common statements you make to customers every day.

Statement 1 ____

____

Statement 2 ____

____

Statement 3 ____

____

Are your statements as positive as they could be? Rewrite the statements to be more positive.

Statement 1 ____

____

Statement 2 ____

____

Statement 3 ____

____

SKILL 4: Using the Customer's Language

Every organization has an internal language. It is loaded with acronyms, buzz words, technical language, and slang. When helping customers, it is important to avoid using this internal language. In every customer conversation, you should communicate clearly and effectively using terms your customer understands.

Language Obstacles

Customer: I'm not clear on this. There's no interest if I paid it off within six months, right?

Rep: Once we process your 501 that's how we'll set it up. You make equal monthly payments to the third party except for the last month, that's the sixth month. For that month their AC will give you the balance and you pay that for your sixth payment. If you have just one delinquency it reverts to a standard APP.

In this example the rep, allowed internal language (501, third party, AC, APP) to dominate the conversation. These unfamiliar terms confuse customers.

Technical language poses a similar problem. If you discuss or explain technical products or services on a regular basis, it is important to keep in mind that customers are more interested in what the product will do for them, not how it works.

Some customers are comfortable with technical language, but others don't understand it nor are they interested in learning it. To determine the customer's level of expertise, begin by giving basic explanations or questions and limited technical language. If the customer is well versed in technical language, it will become clear early in the conversation.

SKILL 5: Gathering Customer Information

A routine part of managing the customer conversation is asking questions to gain information from the customer. It is important to ask the right type of question to get the information you need. Anyone can gather information if given enough time, but successful CSRs know how to ask the minimum number of questions to gather maximum information.

Open and Closed Questions

Two types of questions help you gather information.

Closed questions focus the conversation. These questions produce a short response or a "yes" or "no." *Did, can, have, do, will, would,* and *is* are words that begin closed questions.

Customer problem: *Doesn't understand his bill. Can't figure out why there is a past due amount.*

Closed question: *Do you have your copy of last months bill in front of you?*

This question is designed to get the customer focused on the previous month's billing because that is where the problem began. In most cases, it is best to begin the problem-solving process with an open-ended question. But in some situations, such as this example, a closed question is the best choice.

Open questions determine a customer's need. These questions illicit a customer explanation and begin with how, when, why, what, who, and where. Open questions are more effective than closed when probing for information.

Customer problem: *New product doesn't work. Light comes on but that's all that happens.*

Open question: *Would you please describe how you connected the cables?*

This question will help open up the discussion.

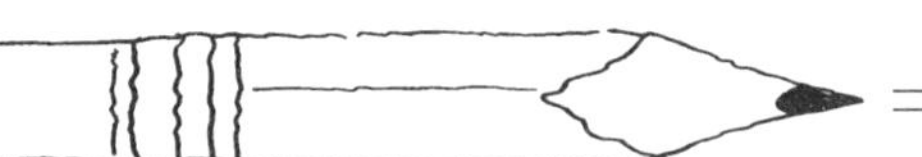

Test Your Knowledge

1. **Circle the words that are used at the beginning of closed qustions.**

   why where did who when is what how do would will can

2. **Circle the words that are usually used at the beginning of open questions.**

   where why did who when how is what will can would do

3. **Write two questions, one closed and one open, that you might ask customers to determine their level of satisfaction with your service.**

   ____

   ____

4. **Write an open question that asks about the weather. Then write a closed question about the weather.**

   ____

   ____

Possible answers:

1. did is do would will can
2. where why who when how what
3. Closed: Are you satisfied with our service?
   Open: How satisfied are you with our service?
4. Open: How is the weather down there?
   Closed: Is your weather still hot?

Keeping It Friendly

When you ask several questions in a row, it is important not to sound as if you are interrogating the customer. The questions can't be asked in rapid-fire sequence. Instead, they need to be "softened" with words like "If you don't mind, please..." and "Will it be okay if...?"

As you ask more questions, these softeners become more important. Softening the questions is an essential skill for CSRs, who often need to gather the same information from every client, such as:

Basic Questions

Your name?

Address and zip code?

Your telephone number?

And your customer number?

These questions can be improved by using the common courtesy we discussed earlier.

Improved Basic Questions

Rep: *May I have your name, please?*

Customer: *Wilma Sanford.*

Rep: *Thank you. And your address please?*

Customer: *2376 Sutter Street, Los Angeles, California.*

Rep: *And the zip code there is?*

Customer: *It's 93923.*

Rep: *Thank you. And may I have a telephone number where we can reach you if we have any further questions?*

Customer: *It's 555-676-2389.*

Rep: *Thank you.*

EXAMPLES OF OPEN PROBING QUESTIONS

These questions draw general explanations of the customer's need:

When did this problem begin?

How did it begin?

When you first noticed the problem, how did it look?

What was the condition of the shipment when it arrived?

How do you think we could best resolve your concern?

What would you like me to do?

Why did they do that?

When you shut the program down, tell me what happens?

Who did you talk with?

Where was the equipment first installed?

CREATING PROBING QUESTIONS

List the five most common customer problems or situations you face and create a question (either open or closed) to begin the conversation.

Common Customer Problem	Your Opening Question
1. ______________________	______________________
______________________	______________________
2. ______________________	______________________
______________________	______________________
3. ______________________	______________________
______________________	______________________
4. ______________________	______________________
______________________	______________________
5. ______________________	______________________
______________________	______________________

The mix of using both open and closed questions can be very effective. Think of it as a "funneling" process. The customer has a concern and you ask open questions to learn about the situation and then follow with closed questions to focus the conversation. The funnel concept is valid because at the bottom of the funnel the solution comes out.

SKILL 6: Satisfying the Angry Customer

A great deal has been written about how to calm an angry customer. There are multiple-step plans, various techniques, and the sage advice, "Stay calm and don't take it personally." The angry customer's dissatisfaction usually stems from one of three factors: management policies, structure of service, or the actions of front-line personnel. The customer sees one or more of these factors as obstacles to his satisfaction.

Hurt Feelings

We may not like to admit it, but most of us have our feelings hurt by angry customers. The exceptions are reps who have learned to not to take the words of angry customers personally.

If customers are upsetting you, you can take steps to decrease the hurt feelings.

STEP 1: Tell yourself the angry customer is upset with your organization not with you.

STEP 2: When your feelings are hurt, respond logically, not emotionally.

STEP 3: Force yourself to remain positive in your comments during the conversation with the upset customer.

Assertive CSRs are less likely to get their feelings hurt due to an angry customer. As we discussed earlier, assertive people tend to be direct and focused on action. They are not very interested in the people side of things. Assertive behavior serves these CSRs well when they are confronted with a highly assertive or angry customer. They refuse to get involved emotionally in the conversation.

If your behavior is assertive, angry customers may not be difficult for you. They are assertive and so are you. As an assertive rep, you need to keep your assertiveness under control. Don't match the customer's assertiveness. Modify your behavior and be patient, understanding, and listen attentively.

Is the Customer Really Angry?

If your behavioral style is not assertive, you need to be aware of a different set of problems. Assuming an assertive customer is angry is a common mistake. But, they may not be angry. To understand this situation, read the following hypothetical interview with an assertive customer.

Rep: *Why are you so angry?*

Assertive Customer: *I'm not angry. I just want action. I know I'm a little demanding, but that's just the way I am.*

Rep: *Do you realize that when we talk there is never any social conversation?*

Assertive Customer: *Why would we have any social conversation?*

Rep: *To be friendly and develop good rapport.*

Assertive Customer: *I don't want to be friendly, and I'm not interested in building rapport with you.*

Rep: *I've always provided you with good service.*

Assertive Customer: *That's true. Is this going to take much longer?*

Rep: *Just a couple more questions, if you don't mind.*

Assertive Customer: *(silence)*

Rep: *When we talk, I feel like we are racing to finish the conversation. Why is that?*

Assertive Customer: *I'm in a hurry. I have a lot of work. I talk fast because I want to get things done.*

Rep: *When I tell you we can't do something you want, you seem to get angry immediately.*

Assertive Customer: *I'm not angry. I just want things my way. I understand "no" better than most of your customers. Look, I've got to go. (click)*

The assertiveness you hear from this type of customer is not anger. You should respond by being more direct, picking the pace up, and keeping the details to a minimum. Listen closely to the next customer you think is angry. Is this customer angry or just being assertive? The answer may surprise you.

Six Ways to Satisfy an Angry Customer

When a customer is truly angry, not merely assertive, there are several actions you can take to help diffuse the situation. Keep in mind that several factors may be at work and that a seemingly small problem may be escalated by other circumstances.

The Irate Customer

Management policy says no refunds after 30 days. The customer calls on the 35th day to demand a refund. Following several minutes of waiting, followed by recorded voice messages and an employee who couldn't help, the customer is becoming angry. The service structure hasn't worked for this customer. Next, you tell the customer there are no exceptions to the refund policy. In this situation the customer might see policies, service structure, and the actions of front-line personnel as obstacles to getting what she wants.

How do you satisfy this customer? Perhaps you won't be able to, but you must try. Taking any or all of the following actions will help make it easier for you to help angry customers.

- ➢ **Act in a courteous manner**
- ➢ **Remain businesslike**
- ➢ **Avoid the customer's emotion**
- ➢ **Apologize for the customer's dissatisfaction**
- ➢ **Explain why (if necessary)**
- ➢ **Offer or mention other benefits**

Act in a Courteous Manner

Every customer, happy or angry, is entitled to courteous treatment. When confronted with genuine courtesy and civility, most angry customers will calm down. It may take a few minutes for this to happen, but it will. It's difficult for most people to be uncivil when treated with civility.

Remain Businesslike

If you become emotionally or personally involved, it's difficult to stay focused on business. As long as you remain businesslike, you have an opportunity to turn a customer from angry to calm. You lose that opportunity when you lose your focus on business.

Avoid the Customer's Emotion

While all the actions can help calm an angry customer, avoiding the customer's emotion is probably most important for the rep. Customers can be rude and overbearing, but you can't join the customer in his emotional swamp. Imagine that the angry customer is an alligator in a dark and hideous swamp. The last thing you want to do is get in the swamp with him.

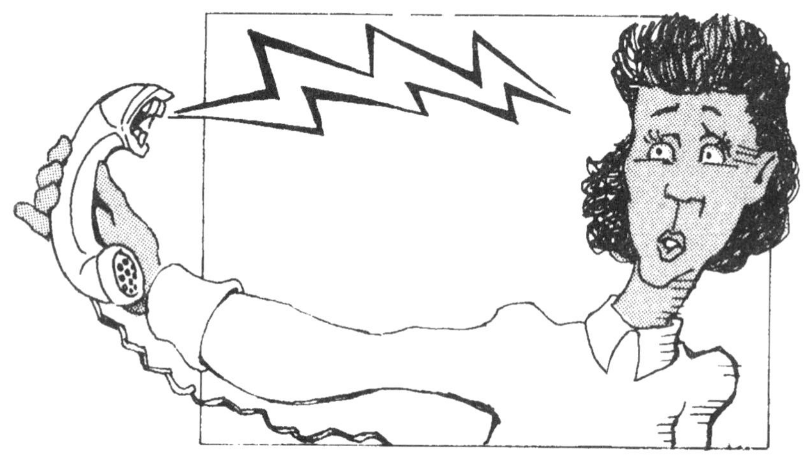

Apologize for the Customer's Dissatisfaction

No matter how angry or how right or wrong the customer may be, an apology is usually in order. You can apologize in a general way or to apologize specifically for something that was done or not done.

General apologies:

"I am sorry you feel that way."

"I'm sorry about this situation."

"I apologize for this situation."

"I am sorry that you are upset about this."

"I feel bad that you are upset about this."

More specific apologies:

"I don't blame you for being upset. I would be too."

"I am very sorry about your bill. I thought we had corrected it."

"I apologize for this situation. We'll get this straightened out right away."

"Please accept my apology for the misunderstanding."

"It is our fault and I am sorry we didn't do what we said we would."

Angry or upset customers like to hear apologies, and they have a calming effect. When the customer has a valid reason to be upset, make a specific apology. When the customer is wrong, you can apologize in a general way to create good will and help calm the situation.

Explain Why (If Necessary)

Analytical customers, more than others, like to hear what went wrong. When customers demand an explanation, be careful with your answer. You should not share internal information that produces a negative image of you and the organization. Instead, offer general explanations, such as these:

> *"There were unexpected delays."*
>
> *"I'm sorry, we simply made a mistake."*
>
> *"I'm not sure what happened, but I can assure it will be straightened out to your satisfaction."*
>
> *"I'm sorry. The information I gave you was incorrect."*

Your customer does not need to know that shipping is understaffed, that marketing's estimate was incorrect, or that your co-workers didn't do what they said they would. These are internal problems and should not be shared with customers.

Offer or Mention Other Benefits

Offering benefits can help calm an irate customer. Even simple benefits, like extra service, can fit the bill. For example: "Would you like me to call you the next time we have a special?" Or, "Our new catalogs just came out. I'll send you one and highlight the new ordering procedure for you. Will that be helpful?"

Your organization's commitment to customer satisfaction is also a benefit you can use to calm upset customers. "I am sorry this happened. We enjoy a reputation for excellent customer service and I hope you will give us another opportunity to prove that to you."

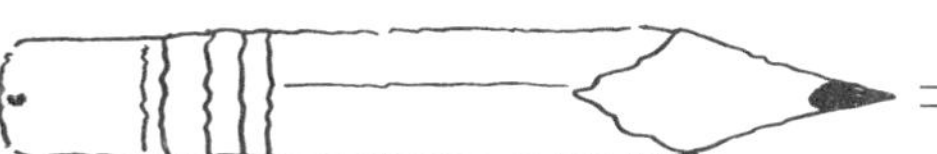

Managing the Angry Customer

Considering the six actions that help manage an angry customer, write your responses to the following customer statements.

1. **Customer statement:** I can't believe this. It's just a couple of days beyond the limit and you won't give me a refund.

   Your response: (Offering a general type of apology may be a good place to start.)

   ____

   ____

2. **Customer statement:** Who do I have to talk with to get this refund?

   Your response: (Remain courteous and explain there is no one else to talk with.)

   ____

   ____

3. **Customer statement:** You don't understand. I must have this refund. Do you realize I have ordered from you before?

   Your response: (Thanking the customer for past business might be an appropriate response.)

   ____

   ____

4. **Customer statement:** I want you to understand that I'm not very happy about this situation and I don't plan on ordering from you again.

   Your response: (Perhaps it's time to offer a final apology and a mention a benefit.)

   ____

   ____

Possible Answers: Managing the Angry Customer

1. **Customer statement:** I can't believe this. It's just a couple of days beyond the limit and you won't give me a refund.

   Possible Response: *I'm sorry about this. We gladly make refunds within a 30-day period, but once that period is over we just can't do it.*

2. **Customer statement:** Who do I have to talk with to get this refund?

   Possible Response: *There isn't anyone else to talk with. Refunds have to be requested within 30 days. I wish I could help you with this, but I can't.*

3. **Customer statement:** You don't understand. I must have this refund. Do you realize I have ordered from you before?

   Possible Response: *Yes, I know you have used our services before. We appreciate your business, and we certainly want to continue to do business with you.*

4. **Customer statement:** I want you to understand that I'm not very happy about this situation and I don't plan on ordering from you again.

   Possible Response: *Again, please accept our apologies. As I said, we appreciate your business and would like to have you as our customer in the future. We seldom have this type of problem. In the future, I think you will be satisfied with our services.*

SKILL 7: Managing Technology

In today's business world, you have multiple ways to communicate with a customer. During a typical workday, you may use the telephone, voicemail, fax, or participate in a customer conference call. Each of these services is easy to use and will be most successful if you follow a few commonsense guidelines.

Telephone

Your telephone is pretty basic isn't it? Just pick it up and talk with the customer. Every business telephone has multiple features, but most reps only use a few features.

YOUR TELEPHONE'S FEATURES

Check (✔) the features below that you need to understand and be able to use. On a scale of 1 to 5, how do you rate your ability to use these features?

1= Poor 3 = Average 5 = Expert

Features You Use	Your Skill Rating
❑ Placing a call on hold	_____
❑ Transferring a call	_____
❑ Transfer a call with an announcement to the receiving individual	_____
❑ Setting up a three-way conference call	_____
❑ Transferring the call back to the attendant	_____
❑ Call pick up	_____

If your rating is less than 5 for any of the features you use on the job, it is time to do a little practicing. Read the documentation for your system or get help from a co-worker who has more experience. The time to practice is now, not when you have a customer on the phone.

Voicemail

Voicemail is a great productivity tool. Customers have come to accept it, but they don't necessarily like it. Here are some common customer complaints about the way many systems are set up.

> *"The options menu seems to go on for a long time before it gives me a choice of connecting with a rep."*
>
> *"Before I connect with my rep, we go back and forth on voicemail a few times."*
>
> *"When my rep isn't available, I would like to be transferred to a rep that can help me."*
>
> *"I understand that a rep can't always be available. But, the rep's personal message should tell me exactly when I can expect a callback."*
>
> *"I have to hold for several minutes and listen to messages before I get a rep who can help me."*

As these complaints indicate, voicemail systems aren't perfect. It is important to understand how your customers feel about your voicemail system. Are there delays? Too many announcements? Are too many messages going back and forth before you finally speak with a customer?

When delays occur a simple apology is in order:

> *"I'm sorry you had to wait so long. How may I help you?"*

When you haven't connected with a particular customer, another simple apology is in order:

> *"My apology for the delays you experienced. How may I help you?"*

Here are some tips for making your voicemail more customer-focused.

Tips for leaving messages:

- When leaving messages for a customers, let them know when you will be available to make it easier for them to reach you when they call back
- Keep the message brief and to the point. Introduce yourself and immediately explain why you are calling.
- When leaving a call-back number, say the number slowly so the customer has time to write it down.
- Repeat your name at the end of the message. This prevents the customer from having to replay the message if he did not catch your name the first time.

Tips for receiving messages:

- Upon returning to your desk, check for messages and return customer calls promptly.
- When you are gone for longer periods, forward your calls to someone who can help the caller, or leave instructions within your greeting stating how the caller can get help.
- Change your personal greeting often so customers will know when they can expect a callback.

Your Personal Greeting

Your personal message should include these eight elements:

1. Your name
2. Work unit ("Customer Service")
3. The date
4. When you will return
5. Instructions for the customer to leave a detailed message
6. When the customer can expect a call from you
7. An alternative for the customer in case it's an urgent situation
8. A courteous ending ("Thanks for calling")

Sounds like a lot of information, doesn't it? But it only takes a few seconds to include all eight elements in your message and doing so will ensure good customer service. With a just a little effort you can easily alter your personal messages throughout the week.

Recognizing a Good Greeting

Rate the following voicemail messages, according to this scale:

E = Excellent G = Good P = Poor

Personal Message 1

You have reached Bob Estes in customer service. I am either on the phone or away from my desk. Please leave me a detailed message and include a good time to call you back. If this call is urgent, you may dial 0 and ask the attendant to page me. Thanks for calling and I'll return your call shortly.

What do you think of Bob's personal message? Not bad, right? Does it sound like yours? Does it include the eight elements?

Your rating ____________

Personal Message 2

Good morning, you have reached Penelope Miller in customer service. Today is Thursday the 12th. I will be away from my desk this morning until eleven o'clock. I'll return your call after eleven. Please leave a detailed message and specify a good time to call you back. If your call is urgent please dial extension 315 and speak with Bob Estes. Thanks for calling and I look forward to talking with you.

Pretty good, don't you think? Do your messages sound like this?

Your rating ____________

Personal Message 3

Hi. This is JoAnn Thomas in customer service. Sorry I missed your call, but leave a message and I'll call you back shortly. Thanks for calling.

JoAnn left out a few factors. Your messages never sound like this, right?

Your rating ____________

Answer Key: Recognizing a Good Greeting

Message 1 is good. To be excellent it needed to include when the customer could expect a callback from it.

Message 2 is excellent. It includes the right information.

Message 3 is poor because there isn't enough information. Unfortunately a lot of voicemail personal messages sound just like Message 3.

Keep in mind that your voicemail response is part of customer communications. Just as you try and satisfy the customer when talking on the telephone, your personal voicemail message should try and do the same.

Fax

When writing fax messages to customers, use business language, keep it brief and to the point, and use the common courtesy of a business letter format.

> Julio sent his customer a routine fax confirming some technical specifications. The fax was brief and to the point, but Julio added a postscript: "P.S. Good luck in your job interview."

Julio's intention was to wish his customer good luck, but he did not use good judgment. Where is your fax machine located? Is it placed where nearly anyone could look at incoming messages? Keep in mind that faxes are seldom private.

Stacy promised a customer she would send the advanced product information if she could get permission from her supervisor. Her fax read like this:

> I am sorry that I will not be able to send the advanced product information. My supervisor said the information is only available to our large accounts at this time.
>
> Thanks for your business.
>
> Stacy

Obviously, Julio and Stacy made mistakes in their faxes to their customers. The point is, be careful what you send to customers and also watch closely how you word messages. As a rule, assume that at least three people will read your fax messages.

Using a Cover Sheet

Some basic information should be built into your fax letter or included on a cover sheet. If your organization does not have a standard fax cover sheet, make one of your own. Include this information:

- Your name
- Name of your organization
- Date
- Your fax number
- Telephone number
- A subject header
- You may want to include your email address as a contact option for the customer to use
- Number of pages being sent, so recipient can be confident of receiving the entire message

Keep in mind that the fax machine may be centrally located and that messages may be picked up and distributed by others. Therefore, include important recipient information such as:

- Recipient's name
- Job title or department
- Phone number

Conference Calling

Conference calling can be an easy way to communicate. There are just a few rules to follow:

- Know how to expertly establish the call.
- When the customer is participating in the conference call, make certain others on the call know it. "John, I have Mr. Michaels on the call with us."
- Introduce the customer to your co-workers "Mr. Michaels, this is John Garcia from our technical support team."
- Encourage the customer to participate rather than just listening. "Mr. Michaels, we are anxious to know what you think about this process–will it work for you?"
- Drop the co-workers from the call before saying goodbye to the customer. "Thanks for spending this time with us John. I will check back with you after Mr. Michaels and I have wrapped things up here."

During the call you have a responsibility to control the conversation between co-workers and your customer. If necessary, you may have to be the customer's advocate as well.

SKILL 7: Managing Technology (CONTINUED)

Marcy established a call between her customer and co-worker Bob Works, an engineer. This is what she said.

"Mr. Customer I'm going to conference in one of our engineers, Bob Works. He will answer the questions you have asked. Will that be all right?"

The conference is established and Marcy says, "Bob this is Marcy from customer service. I have Mr. Customer on the call with us. Mr. Customer this is Bob Works, one of our engineers." They exchange greetings.

Marcy then says, "Mr. Customer is interested in the reliability study we conducted at our beta sites. Bob, will you tell Mr. Customer briefly how we set up the study and what the overall results were? He's especially interested in the test procedures."

The conversation goes on and Marcy encourages the customer to ask questions. She also keeps the conversation focused by asking questions for the customer.

When the conversation ends Marcy says, "Bob thanks for your help. Mr. Customer I'll drop Bob from the call and we can talk for a minute."

Marcy disconnects Bob and talks with her customer for a moment before saying goodbye.

Marcy managed the conference call very well. It is just a matter of following a few basic guidelines.

SKILL 8: Writing Effective Email

Some call centers rely on email almost as much as the phone for customer communications. CSRs are spending much more time receiving and responding to customers via email. It is important to recognize that personal email is different from business email. Our personal email is usually casual and we seldom pay attention to spelling, punctuation, grammar, or format. When emailing a customer, this casualness must be avoided.

EMAIL ETIQUETTE

- Request the customer's permission before sending an email
- Like a business letter, include from, to, date, and subject
- Begin with the same salutation you would use in a business letter
- Be brief and to the point
- Use common courtesy
- Review attachments carefully
- End the email by thanking the customer for his business

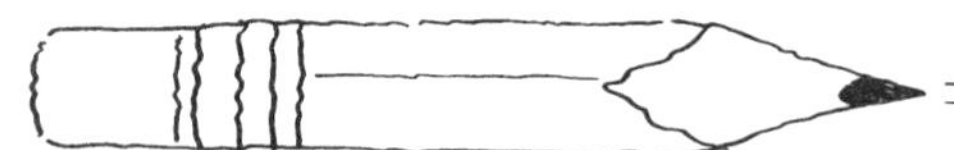

Assess Your Email Aptitude

Test your email knowledge by reading the following statements and marking each as either T for true or a F for false.

1. ____ **It is okay to use my organization's email for personal messages.**
2. ____ **Most organizations have a stated email policy.**
3. ____ **Emails are always private.**
4. ____ **Email should be polished before being sent to a customer.**
5. ____ **Emails should be short and to the point.**
6. ____ **Acronyms, internal language, buzz words, jokes, and slang should not be used in emails to customers.**
7. ____ **Customer emails should be proofread before being sent.**
8. ____ **Customer should be given the choice to be contacted by telephone or email.**
9. ____ **In customer emails, jargon is appropriate.**
10. ____ **Smileys and other humorous graphics are okay to use with customer email.**

Answers: 1. F 2. F 3. F 4. T 5. T 6. T 7. T 8. T 9. F 10. F

Attaching Documents or Other Files

Attachments are often included with email. Pages from your catalog, tech support information, price lists, copies of letters, product descriptions, and an assortment of other information is sent to customers through attachments. In many situations, it is easier to include documents "as is" rather than extract the relevant information the customer wants. However, there can be risks if you aren't careful.

Review documents through the eyes of a customer; make sure the content and wording are appropriate and present a positive impression for your organization.

John's customer wanted an explanation of the warranty she had received with her new DVD Player. John located the warranty information and emailed it to the customer. Included in the information was a memo from engineering suggesting that the warranty period be reduced on certain models because of the performance problems with the new chip.

Everything you email a customer needs to be carefully examined first. Emails don't have to be as formal as a business letter, but they must contain the basics of good customer communications.

Email Exercises

Exercise 1

Starting with the subject, rewrite this email. Make it clear, brief, and to the point.

From: Alpha Inc. Jackie Brown
To: Anderson Co. Attention: Ron Wilson
Sent: August 9, 2000 11:16
Subject: I got the new pricing

The new packet pricing is $49.99 per unit. A discount of 10% applies with the purchase of 10 or more units. You can get up to 20% off with the purchase of 30 units. Let me know what you want to do.

Your rewrite:

Subject ____

____

____

____

____

____

____

____

____

____

CONTINUED

CONTINUED

Exercise 2

This time your task is to reduce the length of the customer email by removing unnecessary information. Draw a line through the unneeded sentences in the email.

From: Alpha Inc. Jackie Brown
To: Anderson Co. Attention: Ron Wilson
Sent: August 6, 2000
Subject: June bill explanation you requested

Dear Mr. Wilson,

My apologies for the confusion regarding your June 9th bill. The following will answer the questions you asked. We billed you for five items. Let's talk about the first one. The first item on your bill is the book, *The New Tax and You.* We showed a $23.95 price for this book. I don't know where we came up with this price. The price per book is $19.95. I have credited $4.00 to your account. The second item was the 100 special bookmarks. We billed a price of $1.00 each. The price is .50 per bookmark. I have credited $50.00 to your account. Again, I'd like to take this opportunity to apologize for our errors. Ever since we changed to the new software we have had some billing errors. The other items on the bill, the covers, the calendars, and the book lights, were all billed correctly. At least we got something right!

Answer Key: Email Exercises

Exercise 1

Here is one rewrite that is more businesslike and professional.

Subject: Requested packet pricing from Alpha Inc.

Dear Mr. Wilson.

The pricing you requested is as follows. Each packet is priced at $49.99. A 10% discount applies with the purchase of 10 or more units. This lowers the price to $45.00. If you purchase 30 units or more a 20% discount applies, lowering the price to $39.99.

I look forward to hearing from you. Thanks again for your business.

Jackie Brown

Exercise 2

Dear Mr. Wilson.

My apologies for the confusion regarding your June 9th bill. The following will answer the questions you asked. ~~We billed you for five items.~~ *(The customer already knows this)* ~~Let's talk about the first one.~~ *(not needed)* The first item on your bill is the book, *The New Tax and You*. We showed a $23.95 price for this book. ~~I don't know where we came up with this price~~. *(makes your organization sound a little stupid.)* The price per book is $19.95. I have credited $4.00 to your account. The second item was the 100 special bookmarks. We billed a price of $1.00 each. The price is .50 per bookmark. I have credited $50.00 to your account. ~~Again, I'd like to take this opportunity to apologize for our errors.~~ *(One apology is usually enough)* ~~Ever since we changed to the new software we have had some billing problems~~. *(This is an internal problem. Don't share it with customers.)* The other items on the bill, the covers, the calendars, and the book lights, were all billed correctly. ~~At least we got something right!~~ *(Don't put your organization down)*

Deleting seven sentences makes the message easier to read, more businesslike, and more professional.

SKILL 9: Mental Scripting

Mental scripting is the process of preparing, practicing, and memorizing a complete response based on a particular statement, question, or objection from the customer. Throughout the day a rep hears the same questions or comments from customers. Customers ask about the cost, the timing, the terms, and so on. Mental scripting means presenting this "everyday information" in a clear and consistent manner.

Mental scripting isn't intended to take away a CSR's individuality. The goal is to get all the needed information out in an organized manner. What about all those product and service descriptions you deliver multiple items per day? Wouldn't it be easier if they were scripted as well? If you want to provide a thorough and easy description, mental scripting makes a lot of sense.

Think for a moment about your co-workers. Is there one who stands out for his or her ability to talk and always seem to have the right response at the right time? Perhaps this person mentally scripts standard responses. To say the right thing at the right time and provide the best possible descriptions and explanation just takes a little preparation.

For example, suppose there are three facts you would like every customer to know about your tech support group. First you want them to know the group is staffed six days a week 12 hours a day. Second, that each tech support employee holds a least a B.S. or equivalent in computer science, and for 90 days following purchase there is no charge for tech support service.

The ideal situation would be for each rep to deliver this information in a concise manner to every customer who asked about tech support services. It might sound like this.

Rep: "We think our technical support is second to none. It's available six days a week, 12 hours a day and all our personnel have degrees in computer science. Our warranty includes free technical support for 90 days."

Examples of Mental Scripting

Customer: *"What does it cost?"*

Simple response: *"It is $26.95."*

Scripted response: *"The cost is only $26.95 and that includes a two-year warranty. We also have volume discounts available for larger orders. How many do you think you will need?"*

Customer: *"When can you deliver it to me?"*

Simple response: *"It will take about seven or eight business days."*

Scripted response: *"The standard delivery is seven to eight days but if you prefer we can overnight it to you or provide a two-day delivery. Which do you prefer?"*

Customer: *"I looked at your catalog but I didn't see anything about racks to hold copper pots."*

Simple response: *"Look on page 59."*

Scripted response: *"There's a good selection of pot racks beginning on page 59."*

Customer: *"I don't seem to understand. Can you explain it again?"*

Simple response: *"Sure." (followed by an explanation)*

Scripted response: *"I'd be glad to. It can be a little confusing. Let's start at the beginning."*

Mental scripting isn't intended to remove the individuality from the rep's response. The goal is to get all the needed information out in an organized manner.

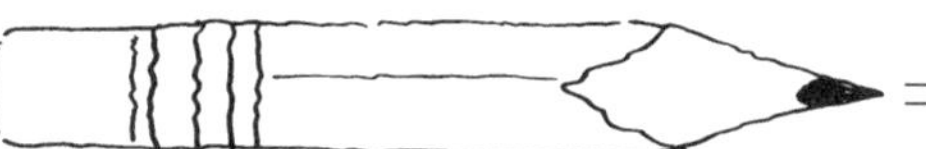

Scripting Your Responses

As you can see it's pretty easy to create a mental script. The best way to get started is to make a list of the most common customer questions, objections, or statements that you encounter.

For each question, objection, or statement, design a mentally scripted response. Keep it short and to the point and, when possible, add a customer benefit.

Customer statement: ______________________________

Scripted response: ______________________________

____

Customer statement: ______________________________

Scripted response: ______________________________

____

Customer statement: ______________________________

Scripted response: ______________________________

____

Customer statement: ______________________________

Scripted response: ______________________________

____

Customer statement: ______________________________

Scripted response: ______________________________

____

SKILL 10: Closing the Conversation

As you finish your telephone conversation, there are some appropriate and courteous statements that should always be made. You should:

- Thank the customer for calling.
- Let the customer know you appreciate his or her business.
- Provide assurance that any promises will be fulfilled.
- Leave the customer with a positive feeling.

Courteous Closing Statements

"Thanks for calling. We appreciate your business."

"Thanks for your order."

"Please call us anytime."

"I enjoyed talking with you."

"Thank you for your patience. I am glad we could resolve your concern."

"It was a pleasure talking with you."

"If you have additional questions, please call us."

"I am glad we were able to help you. Please call again."

"I know you had to wait a long time. Thank you for being so patient."

"My apology about the mix up. We do appreciate your business."

"Thanks for placing your order with us."

"Goodbye, and thanks for calling."

TIP: Always let the customer hang up first. This is simple courtesy, plus it gives the caller a final chance to add something.

P A R T 5

Attitude —Your Most Important Asset

Shaping Your Attitude

In addition to professionalism and communication skills, a positive attitude is an essential quality for a successful CSR. When you were hired, your attitude may not have been discussed, but it was definitely noted. Your attitude is always on display for co-workers, supervisors, and customers. When preparing for work you either include a positive attitude or you don't. When you bring a good attitude to work, it is welcomed by everyone.

Some people are always upbeat and positive. Others may struggle to present a positive attitude. The most important thing to remember is that you can choose to change your attitude. While outside circumstances may influence your emotions and feelings, you choose whether you will react positively or negatively.

When the alarm clock went off, Raymond awoke tired. His first action of the day was to throw his pillow at the clock, knocking it on to the floor. He fell back asleep and awoke 15 minutes later. He was going to be late if he didn't start moving. The empty milk carton meant no cereal and there was hardly time for coffee. The traffic was a nightmare. A fender-bender near work really slowed things considerably.

Rushing into work, just on time, Raymond ran into his supervisor who growled, "Your activity report is late, again." He sat down at his desk and his telephone rang. Raymond felt like not answering the phone, but he picked up the call. The customer on the telephone was a highly assertive demanding type. Raymond felt like he was racing to answer the rapid-fire questions coming from this customer. The call ended as abruptly as it began. The phone rang again. Raymond shook his head and answered the call. It was going to be one of those days, he thought.

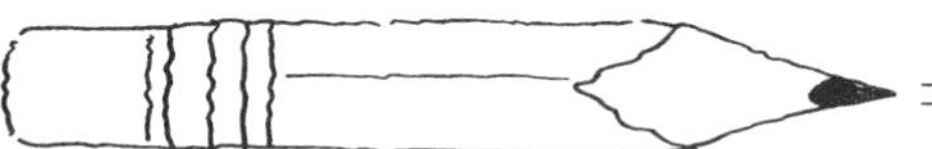

Influences on Attitude

What do you suppose will determine how the rest of Raymond's day goes? Answer this question by checking all of the factors below that might influence Raymond's attitude for the balance of his day.

- ❑ **Raymond's past experience when days started like this one**
- ❑ **His self-talk (Is it positive or negative?)**
- ❑ **His overall feeling of physical and mental well-being**
- ❑ **His sense of humor**
- ❑ **His desire to be positive**
- ❑ **His level of enthusiasm for his work**
- ❑ **His level of self-awareness (regarding his job and environment)**
- ❑ **His motivation to provide quality customer service**
- ❑ **His ability to look at the future rather than the past**
- ❑ **His willingness to select a positive attitude**

Many factors influence attitude. These are some of the most important. Did you check each factor? If you did, you probably recognize that you have choices to make in the attitude you bring to your work as a CSR.

Choosing a Positive Attitude

If you want to improve your attitude, there are a couple of areas you can concentrate on.

- Rather than focusing on negative past experiences, **concentrate on the positive** experience.
- Control your **self-talk** by making it positive.
- Improve your **physical and mental well-being** by exercising and getting enough rest.
- Maintain your **sense of humor.** The ability to laugh at ourselves and not to take our every action so seriously has great therapeutic value as well.
- You have to want a positive attitude. The stronger your **desire to be positive** is, the easier it will be for you to remain positive.
- **Be enthusiastic.** Enthusiasm is contagious. As you act enthused, your customers and co-workers will pick up on it, and everyone's attitude will improve.
- Observe and monitor your own attitude. As you **develop self-awareness,** you will be able to shift your mood from negative to positive quickly.
- The higher your **motivation** the easier it will be to overcome negative situation and feelings.

What Is Your Attitude Toward Customers?

Take this quiz to see how your customer attitude measures up. Respond to each statement with T for true or F for false.

1. ____ **It is reasonable for customers to expect me to know everything about our products and services.**
2. ____ **Customers have the right to expect quality service every time they call.**
3. ____ **If customers knew how many calls I managed each day and how much work I did, they would be more patient.**
4. ____ **Customers can't tell when my attitude is negative.**
5. ____ **My self-talk has a lot to do with how I treat customers.**
6. ____ **Those highly-assertive, demanding type customers are just jerks.**
7. ____ **It is reasonable to expect me to be highly motivated to provide quality service with every customer call I get.**
8. ____ **Some days just go wrong. On those days this idea of selecting a positive attitude just won't work.**
9. ____ **Customers are too demanding.**
10. ____ **I can't be expected to manage every customer conversation.**

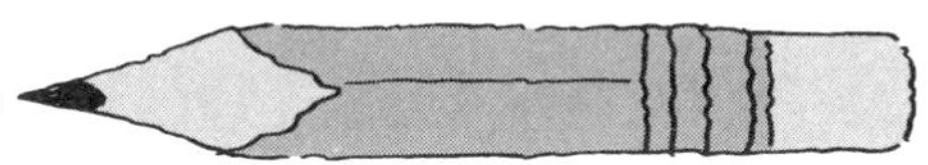

Answer Key: What Is Your Attitude Toward Customers?

1. **True.** Customers have every right to expect that you will know everything about the products and services you offer. In their minds you are the expert.
2. **True.** As an organization, and as a CSR, you want your customers to hold high expectations about your quality service.
3. **False.** Why should customers care about your workload or your problems? They have their own work and problems, and they are calling you for help.
4. **False.** Any negative attitude comes across to customers *and* co-workers.
5. **True.** The more positive your self-talk, the more positive you will be toward customers.
6. **False.** Highly-assertive, demanding customers can act like jerks, but they are your customers. They deserve your respect.
7. **True.** Being highly motivated to provide quality service with every customer call is part of your job.
8. **False.** Selecting a positive attitude always work, if you let it.
9. **False.** Sometimes customers demand a lot. But, they can't be too demanding.
10. **False.** Yes, you are expected to manage every customer conversation. Your organization expects it and the customer expects it.

The Impact of Stress on Your Attitude

Our bodies and minds work together. If we drain ourselves physically, it can take a toll on our mental capabilities. There is a strong connection between the body and the mind, and that connection means stress can take a toll on your ability to maintain a positive and professional attitude.

Locating the Source of Stress

Morgan was seriously thinking about giving up her call center job. She told her supervisor; "There's just too much pressure and stress. Most days I am completely exhausted by the end of my shift." Her supervisor knew that Morgan's activities included an active social life with minimal amounts of sleep, at times. The supervisor had also observed that Morgan used a lot of caffeine to get going in the morning. She asked Morgan; "Do you think all of the stress you are experiencing is caused by your job or might be there other factors?"

What a great question the supervisor asked! When you experience stress it is important to determine the source. Morgan sees her stress situation as strictly work related, but if she looked more closely at the source of her stress, she might decide that lack of sleep and caffeine use were also contributing.

Reducing Stress

To reduce the amount of stress you feel, you must make changes.

David B. Posen, M.D., an authority on stress management, says that since we cause most of our stress, we can do something about it. To reduce your stress, he recommends that you discover the cause of your stress and make changes.

- Change your behavior
- Change your thinking
- Change your lifestyle
- Change your situation

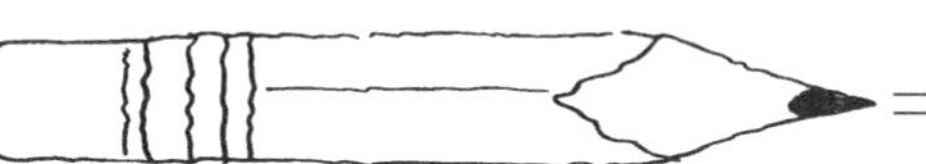

Stress Factors

Stress is often caused by a combination of work- and non–work-related factors.The list below includes job-related and non–job-factors that induce stress. Check (✔) all that may currently be contributing to your stress level. Then make some decisions about how to change your behavior, your thinking, your lifestyle, or your situation to reduce the stress in that may be getting in the way of your positive attitude.

Non–job-related

- ❑ caffeine
- ❑ poor sleep habits
- ❑ financial worries/other personal problems
- ❑ lack of regular exercise
- ❑ diet
- ❑ unrealistic expectations
- ❑ negative attitude
- ❑ smoking
- ❑ alcohol
- ❑ illness/medical concerns
- ❑ people/family/friends
- ❑ living situation
- ❑ behavioral issues: e.g., lack of organization, difficulty concentrating, temper, etc.

Job-related

- ❑ the volume of calls
- ❑ upset/angry customers
- ❑ constant need to update knowledge on products/services
- ❑ the overall workload
- ❑ the fast pace
- ❑ conflict with my co-workers or supervisor
- ❑ personal need for accuracy and correctness
- ❑ office gossip and drama
- ❑ lack of job knowledge
- ❑ don't like my job
- ❑ don't like my organization
- ❑ lack of teamwork
- ❑ the slow pace (decisions and actions take too long)
- ❑ the long commute to work ___

The Call Center Workload

We know that most CSRs experience on-the-job stress due to the demanding workload of customer calls. Let's look at one approach to reducing the impact of these stress contributors.

Sean was pretty calm at the beginning of every workday but as the day wore on he could feel his stress level rise. He decided to ask his friend Patrick, a more experienced CSR, how to avoid this stress. Patrick had some words of wisdom to offer Sean. He said; "We either fight or run from stress." Sean said he didn't want to run from it he just wanted to reduce it. Patrick told him an important key to call center work, and a stress reducer, is keeping up on all the changes (products and services) and focusing on one call at a time. "You can't look ahead to the calls you will manage. You need to focus on the call you're on and when it ends take the next call and focus on it. When we start thinking about all the calls that lie ahead it's easy to feel overwhelmed and that leads to stress." Sean received some very good advice. He considered his personal stress contributors and developed an action plan to reduce his stress level.

Sean's Action Plan

1. Focus on one call at a time.
2. Avoid thinking about future calls.
3. Spend more time learning about the products and services.
4. Try and relax more at lunch and during rest breaks.
5. Get a good night's sleep. (Especially later in the week.)
6. Avoid listening to or participating in the office gossip and drama.

Sean's action plan addresses a combination of personal and work-related factors. Think about the level of stress you feel. If it is low perhaps nothing needs to be done, but if you feel stressed–even for a portion of the day–review your stress contributors. Perhaps you need to design an action plan that will help manage your stress. If you reduce your stress level, you are guaranteed to increase your job satisfaction.

Avoiding Office Gossip and Drama

Did you notice in Sean's action plan that he listed "avoid listening to office gossip and drama"? Drama and gossip can produce a lot of stress.

Sydney heard a rumor about a reorganization of her work group. By late morning everyone was talking about it. She was concerned because she liked her group and didn't want any changes. By late afternoon, Sydney was feeling stressed over the reorganization and left work a little worried. That night she had trouble sleeping. The next day she asked her supervisor when the reorganization might occur. Her supervisor replied, "This is news to me. Where did you hear about it?" Sydney responded, "It's all over the office." The supervisor laughed and suggested that Sydney should quit listening to the rumor mill.

In nearly any office you can find gossip, rumors, and drama. Most offices have staff members who have personally appointed themselves drama king or queen. If you find your stress level or your positive attitude negatively impacted by this drama, you should make a point to avoid it. Make it your policy not to listen or participate in office drama. Keep in mind the old saying: *Gossip and you will be slandered. Mind your own business and you will be respected.*

PART 6

A Plan for Self Improvement

Three Steps to Self Improvement

Developing a plan of action for self improvement is not difficult. However, the implementation requires some discipline and consistent effort. It is worth the effort because it can improve your job performance and your job satisfaction.

Typically we think self improvement is only needed if job performance is low. But self improvement applies to everyone. There is always room for improvement, even for high performers. To create a plan, follow these three steps.

STEP 1: **Take stock of your skills.** Examine and list each skill and knowledge that make up your job performance.

STEP 2: **Define your objectives.** Rate each of your skill and knowledge areas from 1 to 5, 1 being poor and 5 being excellent.

STEP 3: **Develop your action plan.** An action plan should include goals and a timeline.

STEP 1: Take Stock of Your Skills

Before you can start your action plan, you must take stock of your skill inventory. Look over this list of skills, and rate each skill 1 to 5:

1 = Little skill 2 = Some skill 3 = Average skill 4 = Better than average 5 = Excellent

You will use these ratings in your action plan:

____ Managing customer calls
____ Knowledge of products and services
____ Being a team player
____ Remaining customer focused
____ Taking responsibility for behavior
____ Making a commitment
____ Recognizing and managing analytical customers
____ Recognizing and managing assertive customers
____ Overall listening ability
____ Understanding of how and when to use courtesy and civility
____ Recognizing statements to avoid
____ Ability to gather information from customers
____ Ability to manage conversations with angry customers
____ Handling the telephone
____ Managing a conference call
____ Handling the fax
____ Understanding of how to write an effective email
____ Developing mental scripts
____ Closing the conversation
____ Ability to keep a positive attitude
____ Managing stress

Other skills you need for your CSR position:

____ ____

____ ____

____ ____

STEP 2: Define Your Objectives

An action plan is comprised of activities that will lead to self-improvement. Set realistic objectives and activities. Your plan does not have to be complex. Keep your plan basic and doable–as simple as ABC.

A Establish an objective. If you can, quantify your objective. For example, "Reduce order entry errors by 50%."

B List activities that you are willing to participate in that will lead to self improvement. These activities could include putting the ideas and suggestions from this book into practice, reading another book, or watching a training video or CD-ROM. See the Recommended Reading list in the back of this book for ideas.

C For every skill area that you rated below a 3 on the previous page, develop a clear, quantifiable objective.

STEP 3: Develop Your Action Plan

Here is an example of how your action plan should look.

Skill or Knowledge	Objective	Activities
Listening to customers	Become a better listener: Eliminate having to ask customers to repeat themselves.	Read: *The Business of Listening* by Diana Bonet. Use the ideas and monitor your performance for improvement.
Handling the telephone	Be able to use call forward and transfer-to-voicemail features.	Review phone manual and practice using features with the help of a co-worker.
Managing stress	Be able to answer each new call with a refreshed attitude.	Enroll in and complete company-sponsored stress management course.

TIP: Get a second opinion before you start on your action plan. Consider asking your supervisor about your ratings. We often perceive our skills differently from those around us.

Self Improvement Plan

Skill or Knowledge Needing Improvement	Objective	Activities	Completion Date

Recommended Reading

Andrus, Carol. *Fat-Free Writing*. Menlo Park, CA: Crisp Publications, 2000.

Bonet, Diana. *The Business of Listening*. Menlo Park, CA: Crisp Publications, 2001.

Brock, Susan L. *Better Business Writing*. Menlo Park, CA: Crisp Publications, 1996.

Caroselli, Marlene. *Thinking on Your Feet*. Menlo Park, CA: Crisp Publications, 1992.

Chapman, Elwood. *Attitude*. Menlo Park, CA: Crisp Publications, 1995.

Chapman, Elwood. *Winning at Human Relations*. Menlo Park, CA: Crisp Publications, 1989.

Decker, Bert. *The Art of Communicating*. Menlo Park, CA: Crisp Publications, 1996.

duPont, M. Kay. *Business Etiquette and Professionalism*. Menlo Park, CA: Crisp Publications, 2000.

Dyck, George and Merrill Raber. *Managing Stress for Mental Fitness*. Menlo Park, CA: Crisp Publications, 1993.

Finch, Lloyd. *Success as a CSR*. Menlo Park, CA: Crisp Publications, 1998.

Finch, Lloyd. *Telephone Courtesy and Customer Service*. Menlo Park, CA: Crisp Publications, 2000.

Finch, Lloyd. *Twenty Ways to Improve Customer Service*. Menlo Park, CA: Crisp Publications, 1994.

Flynn, Nancy and Tom Flynn. *Writing Effective E-Mail*. Menlo Park, CA: Crisp Publications, 1998.

Fossum, Lynn. *Overcoming Anxiety*. Menlo Park, CA: Crisp Publications, 1990.

Freestone, Julie. *Telemarketing Basics*. Menlo Park, CA: Crisp Publications, 1989.

Freidman, Nancy. *Telephone Skills from A to Z*. Menlo Park, CA: Crisp Publications, 2000.

Goman, Carol Kinsey. *Adapting to Change*. Menlo Park, CA: Crisp Publications, 1992.

Griggs, Rick. *Personal Wellness*. Menlo Park, CA: Crisp Publications, 1990.

Jaffe, Denis T. and Cynthia Scott. *Take This Work and Love It*. Menlo Park, CA: Crisp Publications, 1997.

Lloyd, Sam. *Developing Positive Assertiveness*. Menlo Park, CA: Crisp Publications, 2001.

Martin, William. *Quality Customer Service*. Menlo Park, CA: Crisp Publications, 2001.

Morgan, Rebecca. *Calming Upset Customers*. Menlo Park, CA: Crisp Publications, 1996.

Pokras, Sandy. *Working in Teams*. Menlo Park, CA: Crisp Publications, 1997.

Potter, Beverly A. *Preventing Job Burnout*. Menlo Park, CA: Crisp Publications, 1987.

Scott, Dru. *Stress That Motivates*. Menlo Park, CA: Crisp Publications, 1992.

The Editors. *Achieving Job Satisfaction*. Menlo Park, CA: Crisp Publications, 1994.

Wolfe, Rebecca Luhn. *Managing Anger*. Menlo Park, CA: Crisp Publications, 1992.

CRISP WORLDWIDE DISTRIBUTION

English language books are distributed worldwide. Major international distributors include:

ASIA/PACIFIC

Australia/New Zealand: In Learning, PO Box 1051, Springwood QLD, Brisbane, Australia 4127 Tel: 61-7-3-841-2286, Facsimile: 61-7-3-841-2618 ATTN: Messrs. Gordon

Philippines: National Book Store, Inc., Quad Alpha Centrum Bldg, 125 Pioneer Street, Mandaluyong, Metro Manila, Philippines Tel: 632-631-8051, Facsimile: 632-631-5016

Singapore, Malaysia, Brunei, Indonesia: Times Book Shops. Direct sales HQ: STP Distributors, Pasir Panjang Districentre, Block 1 #03-01A, Pasir Panjang Rd. Singapore 118480 Tel: 65-2767626, Facsimile: 65-2767119

Japan: Phoenix Associates Co., Ltd., Mizuho Bldng, 3-F, 2-12-2, Kami Osaki, Shinagawa-Ku, Tokyo 141 Tel: 81-33-443-7231, Facsimile: 81-33-443-7640 ATTN: Mr. Peter Owans

CANADA

Crisp Learning Canada, 60 Briarwood Avenue, Mississauga, ON L5G 3N6 Canada Tel: 905-274-5678, Facsimile: 905-278-2801 ATTN: Mr. Steve Connolly

Trade Book Stores: Raincoast Books, 8680 Cambie Street, Vancouver, BC V6P 6M9 Canada Tel: 604-323-7100, Facsimile: 604-323-2600 ATTN: Order Desk

EUROPEAN UNION

England: Flex Training, Ltd., 9-15 Hitchin Street, Baldock, Hertfordshire, SG7 6A, England Tel: 44-1-46-289-6000, Facsimile: 44-1-46-289-2417 ATTN: Mr. David Willetts

INDIA

Multi-Media HRD, Pvt., Ltd., National House, Tulloch Road, Appolo Bunder, Bombay, India 400-039 Tel: 91-22-204-2281, Facsimile: 91-22-283-6478 ATTN: Messrs. Aggarwal

SOUTH AMERICA

Mexico: Grupo Editorial Iberoamerica, Nebraska 199, Col. Napoles, 03810 Mexico, D.F. Tel: 525-523-0994, Facsimile: 525-543-1173 ATTN: Señor Nicholas Grepe

SOUTH AFRICA

Alternative Books, PO Box 1345, Ferndale 2160, South Africa Tel: 27-11-792-7730, Facsimile: 27-11-792-7787 ATTN: Mr. Vernon de Haas